T0293355

PERSONAL FINANCE

FROM **SAVING** AND **INVESTING** TO **TAXES** AND **LOANS,** AN ESSENTIAL PRIMER ON **PERSONAL FINANCE** 101

ALFRED MILL

With a Technical Review by Michele Cagan, CPA

Adams Media

New York   London   Toronto   Sydney   New Delhi

Adams Media
An Imprint of Simon & Schuster, Inc.
100 Technology Center Drive
Stoughton, MA 02072

First Adams Media hardcover edition October 2020

ADAMS MEDIA and colophon are trademarks of Simon & Schuster.

For information about special discounts for bulk purchases, please contact Simon & Schuster Special Sales at 1-866-506-1949 or business@simonandschuster.com.

The Simon & Schuster Speakers Bureau can bring authors to your live event. For more information or to book an event contact the Simon & Schuster Speakers Bureau at 1-866-248-3049 or visit our website at www.simonspeakers.com.

Manufactured in the United States of America

7 2024

Library of Congress Cataloging-in-Publication Data has been applied for.

ISBN 978-1-5072-1435-0
ISBN 978-1-5072-1436-7 (ebook)

Contains material adapted from the following titles published by Adams Media, an Imprint of Simon & Schuster, Inc.: *The Everything® Personal Finance in Your 20s & 30s Book, 3rd Edition* by Howard Davidoff, JD, CPA, LLM, copyright © 2012, ISBN 978-1-4405-4256-5; *Debt 101* by Michele Cagan, CPA, copyright © 2020, ISBN 978-1-5072-1266-0.

CONTENTS

CHAPTER 7:

HOUSING OPTIONS 134

CHAPTER 8:

LIVING TOGETHER AND MARRIAGE 174

CHAPTER 9:

THE IMPACT OF TAXES 193

CHAPTER 10:

PLANNING YOUR RETIREMENT 209

INDEX 250

INTRODUCTION

One of the most important things you can do is to get and keep control of your personal finances. Your finances aren't separate from the rest of your life; they provide a structure for you. Once you get a handle on them, you'll feel less stress and more empowerment, and you can set about achieving the goals you want to fulfill. In this book you'll discover that money management isn't complicated; it comes down to being self-aware and disciplined. *Personal Finance 101* gives you advice ranging from how to cut your spending to what kind of insurance you should buy. It offers plans for:

- Debt relief
- Retirement planning
- Budgeting
- Credit issues

Once you've set your personal financial goals, you need to figure out how to fulfill them. This means establishing where you're at and how to get where you need to be. Such a course can mean everything from establishing your net worth to fixing your credit card debt. From life-changing decisions (buying a house) to annual tasks (paying your taxes), arranging your personal finances in an orderly manner can make your life easier.

Personal Finance 101 provides you with a road map to responsible management of your money. When you develop good financial habits, you'll find that it's easy to stay on that road. It may even take you to some exciting places you hadn't anticipated—whether it's traveling to new places or expanding your lifestyle.

Good money management will not only take stress out of your life; it will put many more options within your reach. You'll start by evaluating the state of your finances. From there, you'll learn important financial habits and how they can help you lead a more secure, more productive, and more stable life!

Chapter 1

Your Financial Road Map

The first, and most basic, part of getting your finances under control is setting your goals and taking stock of what you have. Once you've done that, you're in a position to move forward and maximize your financial gains. But first things first!

SETTING FINANCIAL GOALS

What You Want to Achieve

All successful organizations have short- and long-term goals and a written plan for reaching them. If you want to be financially successful, you should have your own goals and plans. The first steps are to determine your financial status today and then decide what you want to achieve for your future and how you're going to accomplish it.

WHY FINANCIAL GOALS ARE IMPORTANT

You wouldn't start out on a long trip into unfamiliar territory without a road map, yet many people go through life without a concrete plan for their financial future. In fact, most people spend more time planning a single vacation than they spend on financial planning. The road you take to financial freedom can lead directly to your destination or to a dead end. Specific financial goals and written plans for meeting them help you focus your efforts on the end result.

Start Early

Starting to save and invest when you're young is a huge advantage. If you invest $5,000 one time at the age of twenty, and that investment earns an average 7 percent interest per year, at retirement (age seventy) you will have over $163,000. The same one-time amount invested at the age of forty would total less than $41,000.

Goals are like the wheels on your car; they keep you moving in the direction you want to go, and you won't get very far without them. If you haven't already started planning for your future, now's the time to begin, no matter what your age.

Saving and investing will give you the most powerful financial tool available: time. In fact, the smartest thing you can do when you're young is save and invest. Ultimately, you'll be able to save and invest smaller amounts at a time and will still come out far ahead of the person who starts a decade or two later. But even as you grow older, developing a clear saving and investing plan will give you a considerable advantage. As the saying goes, "Most people don't plan to fail, they just fail to plan." Without planning, even the best of intentions go nowhere. Start mapping out your route now. Your entire future depends on it.

WHAT'S YOUR NET WORTH?

An Evaluation of Your Finances

As with any road map, before you can determine how to get from here to there, you need to know where "here" is. Where do you stand financially? Answering this critical question is the job of the net worth statement. Your net worth is the difference between all the things of value that you own and all the debts you owe—or, in financial terms, your assets minus your liabilities. Your net worth statement is a list of each of these items and their current value or balance.

WHY YOU NEED A NET WORTH STATEMENT

The net worth statement gives you a snapshot of your financial condition at the current moment. You need this information to effectively set the financial goals you'll be working toward, assess your progress along the way, and make adjustments, using the important clues gleaned from updating your net worth statement on a regular basis. It will also come in handy when applying for a mortgage, credit card, or car loan. Sometimes people avoid making a list of their debts because they're afraid they won't like what they find, or they believe they already have a good "gut feel" for their overall financial picture. However, avoiding your total debt picture can cause major financial damage, and gut feelings can be way off the mark. Not having a handle on your financial condition can seriously hurt you in a time of crisis, such as a job loss or disability, and it's difficult, if not impossible, to plan for the future if you don't know where you are today.

How to Prepare a Net Worth Statement

Start by listing all the things of value that you own, even if you owe money on them, such as your house and car. Use their full market value as of today. The balances of the loans related to these assets will be included in the liabilities section, so your equity (the amount you actually own) in the assets you list won't be overstated. For bonds, stock options, and retirement accounts, use the current value, not the value at maturity or the value on the date you're fully vested. You should receive statements showing the current value of your accounts from your employer for retirement accounts and from your broker for bonds, and most financial institutions offer online account services with values updated daily. The human resources department where you work can help you determine the current value of your company stock options.

List only those life insurance policies that have a cash value. Most life insurance policies are provided by employers and are term policies good only for the time you're employed by that company. These are not considered assets. If you've purchased cash-value life insurance from an agent and you're unsure of the current cash value, she should be able to help you determine the amount you would get if you cashed it in today. Use that amount for your net worth statement.

For cars and other vehicles, use the Kelley Blue Book value, which is the estimated price the car would sell for if sold privately to another consumer or to a car dealer. You can look up Kelley Blue Book values at the library or online at www.kbb.com. For all other assets, use your best estimate of the fair market value.

Assets

- Bank and money market accounts
- Certificates of deposit (CDs)
- Cash on hand
- Stocks, bonds, mutual funds
- Savings bonds
- Other investments
- 401(k)/pension funds
- IRAs (Individual Retirement Accounts)
- Small-business retirement plans
- House
- Land
- Rental property
- Vehicles
- Campers and RVs
- Boats
- Furnishings
- Jewelry and furs
- Electronic equipment
- Rents due you
- Rental deposits (paid)
- Utility deposits (paid)
- Whole life insurance
- Privately owned business

Now you've listed everything you own that has a monetary value, but the total is not a true representation of your financial worth. It doesn't take into account the money you may owe banks or finance companies before you fully own some of your assets—such as your house or car, for example. It also doesn't take into account the money you owe to other creditors. These are called your liabilities.

Liabilities

- Mortgages
- Home equity loans and HELOCs (home equity lines of credit)
- Vehicle loans
- Student loans
- Credit card balances
- Store credit card balances
- Gas credit cards
- Real estate taxes
- Unpaid income taxes
- Quarterly estimated taxes
- Unpaid bills due
- Alimony
- Child support
- Any other money that you owe

Fair Market Value

The fair market value is the price a willing, rational, and knowledgeable buyer would pay. It may be more or less than you paid for the item and is the most meaningful measure of its current worth.

When you've listed everything you can think of, total the assets and then total the liabilities. Now, subtract your liabilities from your assets. If the number is positive (assets are greater than liabilities), you have a positive net worth. Congratulations! Now you can start working on building that net worth. If the number is negative (liabilities are greater than assets), you have a negative net worth, but don't let it discourage you; it's just your starting point. Negative net worth is extremely common, especially for people who've recently entered the workforce. Now that you know exactly where you stand, you can map out your route to a positive net worth.

DECIDE WHAT YOU WANT

Getting a Plan

Setting goals is as simple as deciding what you want and mapping out a plan for getting it. Many people focus on their immediate wants and needs at the expense of their short- and long-term goals. Current expenses have a way of expanding to use all your available money, making future planning and saving seem impossible, but they're not. By focusing on your budget, spending less money than you're bringing in, and keeping a closer watch on credit spending, you'll be able to save, invest, and get ahead.

GO FOR THE GOAL

Think seriously about what you want to achieve. What's important to you? Do you envision retiring while you're still young enough to enjoy travel or an active lifestyle? Would you like to buy your first home or move up to a larger home in a better neighborhood? In the shorter term, maybe a new car or a boat is on your wish list.

If your short-term liabilities (due in a year or less) are greater than your current assets (cash and assets like stocks that can be quickly turned into cash), paying down credit card debt makes a smart first priority.

Don't choose goals just because they sound like what you should want. Ask yourself whether the goals you're setting are worth sacrificing some spending now for the future enjoyment of having what will be really meaningful to you later.

Stretch Goals

Don't let fear of failure cause you to set goals that aren't ambitious enough. You want to stretch yourself a little to reach your goal, but it has to be achievable, or you won't stay motivated for long. Try to strike a balance.

PUT IT IN WRITING

Whatever your goal, simply dreaming about it won't make it happen. A goal should be written down and reviewed regularly. Written goals give you something to work toward and make your efforts to save more meaningful. Figuring out how to achieve your goals is just as important as stating them. When you put a goal in writing, include the following:

- A description of the goal
- The time frame for achieving it
- The amount of money needed
- The amount already saved
- Your plan for achieving the goal (for example, putting aside $100 a month, working ten hours of overtime a week, cutting entertainment costs in half, or getting a second job)

Having a deadline for achieving your goal creates a sense of urgency that makes it easier to stay focused.

Write down your goals in enough detail to give yourself a visual each time you read them. If you're saving to buy a house, don't just write down "buy our own house." Include details so you can almost see it: "I want to buy a cozy Cape-style home with a water view on two or more wooded acres on the coast of Maine." Each time you think of this goal, picture this cozy home in your mind. The more vividly you can imagine what your goal will look like and feel like, the better chance you have of achieving it.

BREAK IT DOWN

At first, what you may have are long-term goals (goals you expect to meet in five years or more). You can break these goals down into short-term goals (one year or less), making it easier to stay focused on the future and giving you a sense of accomplishment and satisfaction along the way. In some cases, you may also want to identify a medium-term goal (one to three years). Remember to make the goals specific. Ask yourself how you'll know when you've reached each of your goals. If you can come up with a concrete, measurable answer, you're on the right track.

After you've written down as many goals as you can think of, choose one or two short-term and one or two long-term goals to work on this year. Let's say you choose building a retirement fund as one of your most important long-term goals. To break it down into short-term goals, set a monthly goal to contribute a set dollar amount to your employer's 401(k) or other retirement plan.

Most people struggle with the question of whether to use available funds to pay down long-term debt, such as making extra principal payments on a mortgage, or to use the money for short-term goals, such as building an emergency fund. The best choice is to figure out which has a higher priority. This takes thoughtful consideration of your current financial situation, your short- and long-term goals, and the flexibility to make adjustments in your plans as your goals and your financial situation change.

EVALUATING YOUR PROGRESS

How Are You Doing?

You've prepared a net worth statement, thought about what you want to achieve in life, identified some goals, and broken them down into short- and long-term goals. Now you need to determine how you'll evaluate your progress.

You may have a sense of whether you're making progress on your goals from month to month, but take the time to sit down regularly (monthly, quarterly, whatever makes the most sense for your situation) and review how you're doing. Long-term goals can be reviewed less frequently than short-term goals because your time frame for achieving them is longer, but more frequent reviews allow you to spot problems earlier and take corrective action if you're falling short of where you want to be.

TIPS FOR RECALCULATING AND REVIEWING

You should recalculate your net worth at least annually, but more frequently is even better. For most people, it only takes a few minutes to update the information once you've generated your first statement. Go over your updated net worth statement, and if you're part of a couple, talk with your spouse or significant other about how much you've accomplished and where you've fallen short. If you're single, you'll do this on your own, unless you want to involve someone else like a close friend or financial mentor. If you're not making satisfactory progress on a particular goal, reevaluate your approach and think about what would help you get on track. If you're making steady progress, seeing it in black and white can be motivating and rewarding. Give yourself credit for what you've achieved so far.

From time to time you may find that your goals have changed, and that's okay. A good financial plan is flexible and changes with your needs. If you lose interest in a goal, don't consider it a failure. There's no reward in working for something you don't really want. Make the necessary changes in your goals and move on.

It can be a tremendous help to engage the assistance of others. Talk to people who have achieved a goal similar to one you're working on. You can gain from their experience and insight, and seeing their success can help keep you motivated.

If you find yourself falling short of your goals because you don't feel motivated enough to stick with your plan, make a list of everything you'll gain once you've succeeded in achieving your goal, and remind yourself often. Don't underestimate the power of your subconscious to help you stay motivated. Put positive thoughts in your mind about your goals, and they'll be easier to attain.

EDUCATING YOURSELF ABOUT MONEY MATTERS

Unfortunately, people don't always learn the basics of personal finance from their parents, and the current education system doesn't adequately teach them either. In fact, the Jump$tart Coalition for Personal Financial Literacy, whose mission is to improve the financial literacy of young adults, says that the average high school graduate lacks fundamental money management skills and a basic understanding of earning, spending, and saving money. It's no wonder that most people make financial mistakes in their twenties and thirties that they pay for over the next decade or longer. You can avoid these mistakes by educating yourself about basic money matters and practicing good money management.

Where to Go for Help

Where do you start? Books like this are one source of reliable information. Check your local bookstore or surf an online bookstore such as *Amazon*, searching for keywords like "personal finance" or "money management." Financial magazines, such as *SmartMoney*, *Barron's*, *Money*, and *Kiplinger's Personal Finance*, are another great source. Some of them are geared toward avid investors or those interested in business financial news, so try several different ones to see if any of them are relatable. If you find one you connect with, consider subscribing to it.

The Internet is a source of nearly limitless information. Try to stick with well-known sites such as *NerdWallet*, *Kiplinger*, and *Investopedia* rather than the "this is how I did it" personal sites. Although the latter can have useful information, these sites can steer you in the wrong direction with some questionable advice or information. On the other hand, the personal sites about frugal living, downsizing, and cutting costs can be great for giving you ideas on how to do the same.

THE BENEFITS OF BUDGETING

Your Road Map

Creating a budget and sticking to it is a crucial part of meeting your goals. Budgeting brings up the idea of cutbacks and sacrifice, but it's really about the opposite: having enough money to afford the things you want without building up debt. A classic budget consists of setting up spending categories, tracking your expenditures, monitoring your progress, making adjustments, plugging spending leaks, and staying motivated. There are different ways to achieve all of that, and you'll find the one that works best for you. Your chances of being financially successful increase substantially once you put a budget in place. It takes a little time and effort to get started, but the rewards are tremendous.

IT'S ALL ABOUT FREEDOM

Budget. For some, the word conjures up images of sacrifice, penny-pinching, and doing without. At least 50 percent of budgeting is mental, so if the word makes you shudder, focus on replacing this negative image with a positive one: A budget means being able to afford a new car, a dream vacation, and a stress-free retirement. If you haven't been able to stick to a budget in the past, that budget system may not have been right for you. It all starts with a plan for every dollar you bring in, and knowing where you want that dollar to go. "Working after the fact" budgeting—looking back at where your money went last month—isn't budgeting. A budget is all about the future.

Why Budget?

A budget is really a money plan. Creating that plan is the first and most basic step you can take toward putting your money to work for you.

Many people who spend more money than they make don't even realize they're spending too much until they're deeply in debt. Spending money without knowing how much you have available can create financial problems, especially when you're using credit cards to cover your spending. Make mindful decisions about your spending by deciding in advance how you want to use your money instead of letting it happen accidentally. When you spend without a plan, you're not in control of your money, and that can leave you with out-of-control money problems.

The Benefits of Budgeting

Budgeting and tracking your expenses show you where your money goes and how seemingly inconsequential daily or weekly expenditures can add up over time. By tracking all of your expenditures, you can make conscious decisions about how to spend, save, or invest your money. This can be the difference between never having enough money and being able to afford the things that are really important to you, such as saving for a down payment on a house, buying a new car, paying off credit card debt, planning for retirement, or saving for that trip to Cancún.

The Benefits of a Simple Lifestyle

The Millionaire Next Door by Thomas J. Stanley and William D. Danko shows that simple lifestyles, not big incomes, turn average people into millionaires. Many Americans buy a more expensive house than they can comfortably afford, drive the newest model of car, spend large sums on their wardrobes, buy all the latest electronic gadgets, and end up living paycheck to paycheck.

Having a working budget can greatly reduce the stress in your life that revolves around money issues. You'll know what you can or can't afford. You'll feel confident that you'll be able to pay your bills when they're due, or you'll have advance warning that there's going to be a problem, giving you time to figure out a way to manage it.

What Makes a Good Budget?

A good spending plan is flexible and realistic. It's a road map that offers alternative routes to your destination, depending on your personal road conditions. It should be dynamic, changing to fit your needs. If you don't have kids, you wouldn't use the same budget as someone who does; if you live in rented housing, you wouldn't use the same budget as someone who owns his home. Life changes, and so should your budget.

The complexity level of a good budgeting system should match the level of your time and interest. Some people love recording the details. If you're not one of them, choose a simpler approach so it's not too much of a chore. The objective is to come up with a system you can live with for a long time.

CUSTOMIZING YOUR BUDGET

It's a good idea to create a worksheet to get started in setting up your budget. This book offers some help for doing that, but make sure the categories you use fit your personal lifestyle. Use the basic common categories that apply to everyone, such as housing, utilities, insurance, and food, but customize the other categories to fit your situation.

Your categories should be detailed enough to provide you with useful information, but not so detailed that you become bogged down in trivia. First, list all your sources of income, making sure to use the amount of money you actually get (take-home pay, for example, rather than gross pay):

- Wages from your job(s)
- Bonuses
- Income from side gigs
- Child support or alimony
- Social Security
- Rental income
- Interest income
- Dividend income
- Capital gains income
- Other income

Next, list the expense categories you want to track. Start out with a little more detail rather than a little less. You can always combine categories later if you find that expenditures in one category are so small they don't warrant being tracked separately.

Some sample expense categories include:

- Emergency savings
- Retirement savings
- Mortgage or rent
- Utilities
- Auto expense
- Other transportation
- Credit card payments
- Student loan payments
- Other loan payments
- Home maintenance
- Childcare
- Child support or alimony
- Insurance
- Out-of-pocket medical expenses
- Computer expenses
- Entertainment/recreation
- Eating out/groceries
- Clothing and shoes
- Gifts and donations
- Hobbies
- Household/personal care products
- Property tax
- Investments
- Pet expenses

Don't forget things that come up throughout the year but are not monthly expenses, such as subscriptions, holiday gifts, birthday gifts, maintenance agreements, car repairs, and so forth.

Pay Yourself First

The first rule of personal finance is to pay yourself first. Make savings your number one expense category, with a set amount that you put aside monthly when you pay your bills. Don't plan your savings around what's left over once you've paid everything else. Chances are there won't be anything left.

Think about your own personal habits (buying lunch at work, going out for drinks with friends) or hobbies you engage in (woodworking, skiing, boating, golfing, gardening) to identify other spending categories. Some of your spending habits might surprise you when you see them in black and white. That's okay. Identifying them just brings them to light so you can make a conscious decision about your spending. The purpose of budgeting is not to make you feel bad or guilty about how you spend your money. It's to make sure you have the money available to spend on the things you want.

OPPORTUNITY COSTS

The Road Not Taken

In addition to immediate missed opportunities, you may also lose out on interest you could have earned by saving or investing that money. On the flip side, you may end up owing more money in interest by not using the money to pay down credit card debt or other loans more quickly. In those ways, spending $100 could end up costing you hundreds—even thousands—of dollars over the long run.

Good Choice or Bad Choice?

Opportunity costs refer to everything you can't use money for once you've spent it. For example, if you spend $100 on a night out with friends, you can't save that $100 toward your new car or use it to pay down your student loans more quickly. It's about the opportunities you miss out on when you spend money. That doesn't mean spending your money that way was a bad choice; it just means you lost the opportunity to use that money a different way once you've spent it.

KNOW WHERE IT'S ALL GOING

Follow the Money Trail

To create a budget you can live with, you need to set realistic spending goals in each category. First, figure out where your money actually goes now. To get started, collect as many of your bills, credit card statements, bank statements, and receipts as possible for the last six to twelve months and total up your monthly spending. Don't forget to include any amounts you direct toward savings, including retirement savings. Once that's done, calculate your average monthly net pay (after taxes and other deductions) by looking at the last six months' worth of take-home pay. Don't include unknown amounts such as year-end bonuses, commissions, or overtime pay. Do include other income amounts you receive every month, like dividends or Social Security. You're figuring out your basic monthly income, so only include money you can always count on.

EVERY EXPENSE COUNTS

In addition to your regular monthly expenses, you want to make sure to include occasional expenditures. For the items you identified that get paid quarterly or annually (or anything other than monthly), calculate the yearly cost and divide it by twelve to get the monthly cost. Include that amount in your monthly expenses to get a more accurate picture of where your money is going. For non-monthly expenses that you know for certain you'll face (like dentist visits), set aside the monthly amount in a savings account so you'll have it handy when you need it.

To really get a fix on where your money goes, you'll need to keep track of your cash expenditures too. Save receipts to record later, or jot the expenditure down on a notepad as you use cash. The more often you use an automated teller machine (ATM), the more important it is to write down your cash expenditures, because this is where many people lose control of where their money goes. Tracking your cash expenditures is one of the tougher aspects of budgeting, but it's also a common source of budget leaks.

Tracking Small Expenditures

Most people are more than a little surprised when they really start tracking their expenses and see where they're spending more money than expected. Small cash expenditures can add up to significant sums of money by month's end. That daily cup of coffee is probably costing you almost $600 a year. Three six-packs of beer a week add up to at least $600 a year. If you smoke two packs of cigarettes a day, it's probably costing you over $280 a month, $3,360 a year, or $33,600 in ten years—and that's if you discount the impact of inflation!

Find Comfortable Ways to Cut Costs

An important part of budgeting is coming up with concrete and relatively easy ways to cut costs. Setting a spending limit with no thought about how to reduce expenses will be an exercise in frustration as you experience monthly shortfalls. Figure out what you can most easily do without to keep more money in your own pocket.

Finding Ways to Reduce Spending

Once you've looked at your actual spending, you'll begin to see a pattern, and will be better able to identify where you can comfortably make adjustments to start saving money. Consider this a process of self-discovery. You can start with an in-depth look at your largest spending categories, and then move on to the smaller categories. Though it might seem like smaller expenditures would be the easiest to cut, mainly because that spending tends to be more discretionary, paring down your largest expenses can make a bigger long-term impact on your budget.

SET SPENDING GOALS BY CATEGORY

Once you feel like you know where your money is going and you've identified some ways to cut costs, establish a realistic monthly spending target for each category. Start with your fixed expenses (amounts that are the same every month), such as your mortgage and car payment. Then look at each of your remaining budget categories and set reasonable spending targets, taking into consideration what you know about your spending habits and where you can cut back without causing a hardship.

Calculating Your Net Income

When you've set a tentative target for each category, add up the total income and expense categories. Then subtract the total expenses from the total income to arrive at your net income; this might be a negative number. If the net is positive, it represents money available for making additional payments on your credit cards, accelerating other debt repayment, bumping up retirement plan contributions, and working on your other financial goals. However much is left over, make a plan for it. Extra cash left in a regular checking account has a way of getting spent.

If the net number is negative, your planned expenses are greater than your income. Don't be discouraged, but do reevaluate your income and expenses. Your situation can be improved by increasing your income and reducing any expenses you can.

MONITORING YOUR BUDGET

Refining and Reevaluating

Once you have a budget in place and are following it (or at least trying to), your next step involves tweaking it. Your first budget is sort of like a first draft, and it may need some editing to fit better with the way your money actually flows in and out. Plus, life changes constantly, and your budget needs to change with it.

MAKING ADJUSTMENTS

If you find you've spent more than you budgeted for the month, don't despair. Use the information as a learning tool to improve your budgeting for the future. Your budget will get more refined every month, and you'll get better and better at managing your money and working toward your goals. If you find after a month or two that tracking every expense is too much work, consider combining some categories, such as miscellaneous household expenses or utilities, to reduce the record keeping, rather than giving up.

As you readjust the categories, look for areas where you can save money. Remember, the idea is not to deprive yourself but to funnel as much of your money as possible toward the goals that are most important to you. As your personal situation changes, reflect those changes in your budget. Examples of changes that should prompt an overhaul of your budget include the following factors:

- Change in marital status
- Change in family size

- A new job
- Salary increase (or decrease)
- A new home
- Disability or chronic illness
- Job loss
- A major purchase that requires monthly payments

PLUG ANY SPENDING LEAKS

Spending leaks can be the result of impulse buying, unused memberships, bank fees, and other small expenditures that add up to a lot by month's end. Impulse spending, or buying things you don't realize you want until you see them, is often the result of powerful advertising messages that are so appealing you buy things you don't need and often end up not using. Forgotten memberships (like a gym or a streaming service) on auto-pay drain your budget every month even though you never use them. Bank fees can really add up, so make sure you know every time the bank pulls money out of your account.

Impulse buying can quickly run up credit card balances, leaving you to deal with debt for a long time. Plan your purchases and don't buy anything on the spot that wasn't part of your plan. If there's something you feel you really must have, think about it for at least two days, and if you still want to buy it, make sure you have enough cash to cover it and do a little comparison shopping first so you don't overpay.

The Small Leaks

Grocery shopping is one area ripe for cost cutting. Do you buy a lot of prepared foods instead of doing the cooking yourself? There's a trade-off between the cost and the convenience of prepared foods when you're too busy to cook. Snacks are another expensive item, especially if you buy the single-serving packages to include in the kids' school lunches. Consider buying family-sized items and repacking single servings into baggies to save money. Other cost-cutting tips to consider include buying generic brands and using coupons whenever you can.

Look for Tech Deals

Shop for phone and Internet service deals twice a year. Media companies are constantly changing their plans, and you could save a chunk of change. Be sure to read the fine print and ask specific questions.

If eating out is a lifestyle instead of a treat, consider cutting back on restaurant food and making more meals at home. Limit dining out to once or twice a month. Those special meals will feel like treats, and you'll end up spending less money.

What's the deductible on your auto insurance? It should be at least $250, and if you have a good driving record, $500 is even better. The certain cost of paying higher insurance for a lower deductible weighed against the likelihood of having an accident is a balancing act. If the car is more than eight years old, consider dropping collision coverage altogether, and just keep liability coverage on that vehicle. The cost of collision coverage on a car that is worth only a few thousand dollars is out of proportion to the benefit you receive, especially if you have a good driving record.

These are just a few ideas to get you thinking about how you can cut costs. As you go through each item in your budget and on your net worth statement, question everything and look at things from a different perspective. Look for ways to save on your biggest expenses—cutting those will free up more money in your budget than reducing a bunch of small expenses.

FIXING THE LEAKS

The Bigger Picture

Once you've reviewed your spending and identified some small spending leaks that you can plug fairly painlessly, start looking for the larger leaks. Review big-ticket items such as your mortgage, car payments, other debt payments, taxes, and insurance policies. It may take some legwork to reduce these expenses, but the payoff will be worth it when you have more room in your budget for the things that are important to you.

How Can Software Make Budgeting Easier?

With personal finance software and apps, you can balance your checkbook, pay bills, track savings and investments, and create budgets. You'll have access to instant reports for things like your planned budget versus actual expenses by category, your net worth, and an up-to-date snapshot of your overall finances.

Personal financial software and apps (like Quicken and Mint) make managing and tracking your finances easier. No need to deal with time-consuming data entry—you can directly link all of your bank, credit card, and investment accounts, and the app or software will do all the work for you.

Shop Around

Many popular personal finance software/apps offer free or trial versions for beginners, with paid upgrades for added features. This gives you the opportunity to try them to see which one works best for you. All of them automate income and track your expenses. Some of the best options to check out include Simplifi by Quicken, Mint, Personal Capital, and YNAB (You Need a Budget).

Where to Find Personal Finance Apps and Software

To try Simplifi by Quicken, visit www.simplifimoney.com; for Mint, go to www.mint.com; for Personal Capital, hit www.personalcapital.com; for YNAB, go to www.youneedabudget.com. For the full version of Quicken software, visit www.quicken.com.

A program like Quicken has many features you may not use right away, but it works well for beginners who just want to do online banking, automatically reconcile their bank statements, track expenses, budget, prepare for tax time, and look at reports. The budget versus actual report alone is worth the investment.

Your budget won't work unless you stick with it. One of the keys to staying motivated is to keep the budgeting process from being too complex or time-consuming. If you're budgeting for a family, make it a family activity and involve each family member in some way; it's a great way to introduce your kids to basic money concepts. Reward yourself for reaching saving and spending goals and making progress on paying down debt.

One of the most rewarding things about tracking your finances is seeing the progress you're making every month. This is easy if you use personal finance software and apps, because they offer a variety of charts, graphs, and reports you can view in real time.

Remind yourself of the importance of your real goals. The budget is just a tool that increases your awareness of where your money goes and provides guidelines for spending so your money goes toward the things that are most meaningful to you.

Chapter 2

How and Why to Save Money

Savings act as the foundation for your financial freedom and security. Even if you feel like there's no room in your budget for savings, it's important to start anyway. Saving just $5 a month is better than saving nothing, and it helps build a savings habit. Any amount you have saved will help you in a time of financial need or crisis. But that all starts with making a savings plan and making savings a top priority expense in your budget.

THE MIRACLE OF COMPOUND INTEREST

How Your Money Grows

Compounding is the way your money grows on its own, and it's the main reason to start saving as soon as you possibly can. Time is your best friend when it comes to compounding, and longer time means a lot more money. That's especially true for long-term savings, like retirement savings. People who wait until their forties or fifties to start saving will have to put away much more than those who began in their twenties.

Compounding

To illustrate the true power of compounding, assume you invest $1,000 at 5 percent interest compounded annually. After ten years, you'd have $1,646. At the twenty-year mark, your account would be worth $2,712. And after forty years, you'd have $7,358. That extra $6,358 is your money working harder for you.

There are two basic methods of calculating interest: simple interest and compound interest. Simple interest accrues (accumulates) only on your initial investment. For example, if you have $1,000 that earns 5 percent simple interest annually, every year your account would grow by $50. With compounding interest, you earn interest on your investment plus the interest it's already earned. For example, if you have $1,000 that earns 5 percent interest compounded annually, you'd earn $50 ($1,000 × 0.05) the first year. The second year, you'd earn interest on your new balance of $1,050, so your interest for the year would come to $52.50 ($1,050 × 0.05). Every year you'd earn interest on interest, helping your money grow that much faster. The effect that compounding can have over a long period of time is astounding, especially with larger initial investments and higher rates of return.

FREQUENCY OF COMPOUNDING

Earnings on saving and investment accounts usually compound annually, quarterly, or monthly. The more frequently compounding takes place, the faster your money will grow. Let's say you put $5,000 in an account that earns 10 percent interest. Here's what your investment would be worth at the end of ten years based on different compounding intervals (and this is without you adding in any more money):

- Compounded annually: $12,968
- Compounded quarterly: $13,425
- Compounded monthly: $13,535

To illustrate the effect of a longer period of time on compounding, consider Bill, who contributed $2,000 at 6 percent interest to an IRA beginning at the age of twenty-two and continued doing so each year until he was thirty-nine. By the time he was sixty-five, his $34,000 investment had grown to nearly $362,000. His friend Jim made a $2,000 contribution every year for thirty-five years, for a total of $70,000, but because he started at the age of thirty-one, his nest egg totaled only about $180,000. Even though he contributed much more than Bill ($70,000 versus Bill's $34,000), he ended up with around 50 percent less money.

THE RULE OF 72

The rule of 72 is a nifty mathematical computation you can use to estimate how long it will take a certain sum of money to double at a certain interest rate (assuming the interest is compounded annually).

The Calculation Is Simple

To calculate how quickly your investment will double, divide 72 by the interest rate or expected rate of return (for earnings other than interest, such as dividends or capital gains). The result is the number of years it will take your money to double, assuming you reinvest your earnings. So if your money is returning 8 percent annually, you make the following quick calculation: $72 \div 8 = 9$. This means it will take approximately nine years for your initial investment to double.

You can also use the rule of 72 to estimate what rate of return you'd need to earn in order for your money to double in a certain number of years; for example, ten years: $72 \div 10 = 7.2$, so you'd need to earn 7.2 percent annually for your money to double in ten years.

As you can see, the real growth comes after the money has doubled several times. By using the rule of 72, you can calculate how much you'll have by a certain time, and you can compare the long-term effects of interest rates on various investments that you own.

Double Savings, Don't Double Debt

You can use the rule of 72 to see how long it will take your credit card or other debt to double too. If you have a $5,000 credit card balance with an interest rate of 10 percent, your debt will double in 7.2 years if you make no payments and no additional charges. If the interest rate is 19 percent, your debt will double in 3.8 years. You can see why it's so hard to pay off your credit card debt, especially if the interest rate is high.

INFLATION IS NOT YOUR FRIEND

Eating Away at Savings

Inflation is the effect of rising prices on your buying power. Inflation is often left out of the equation when calculating how much money you'll have available at some point down the road, but it can make serious inroads into the buying power of your money. In the United States, the average annual inflation rate since 1990 has been approximately 2.5 percent. Since 1990, the price of goods and services has increased 106 percent, so an item that cost $100 in 1990 costs $206 in 2020. Since much of financial planning is done for years into the future, it's important to consider the impact of inflation when determining how much money you'll need in retirement, for example.

The Effects of Inflation

The $30,000 salary you earn this year will be worth only $28,800 in purchasing power next year if inflation is 4 percent. If you're fortunate, you'll get a salary increase annually that at least keeps pace with the rate of inflation; otherwise you fall further behind each year.

You can use the rule of 72 to estimate the real buying power of a sum of money at some point in the future, taking inflation into consideration. If the inflation rate is 4 percent, prices will double in eighteen years ($72 \div 4 = 18$), so if you plan to retire in eighteen years and you need $3,000 a month in today's money, you'd need $6,000 a month to retain the same buying power you have today.

THE TIME VALUE OF MONEY

The time value of money is a basic financial concept based on the assumption that a dollar received today is worth more than a dollar received at some future date because today's dollar can be invested and earn interest. If someone offered to pay you either $1,000 ten years from now or some lesser amount today, you could calculate the amount you'd need to receive today to equal or exceed the value of $1,000 in ten years and decide which is the better deal. You do this by backing into the amount using current interest rates. For example, if the current interest rate is 3 percent, you might be willing to accept $744 today rather than waiting ten years for your $1,000 because you're confident interest rates will stay level or increase over the next ten years.

BUILDING AN EMERGENCY FUND

Your Backup Money

Everyone should have an emergency fund, but you probably won't know how much your fund should be unless you know what your basic monthly expenses are. Financial advisors usually suggest having enough savings in an easily accessible account to cover your living expenses for three to six months, but it's not a one-size-fits-all situation. Depending on the number of breadwinners in your household and your other sources of cash, your family may need more than six months of expenses in an emergency savings account. Having this financial safety net will give you peace of mind about how you'll meet your most basic financial obligations in the event of illness, job loss, unplanned expenses such as major house or car repairs, or medical costs not covered by insurance. If you're uncertain about your job and the job market, an emergency fund is especially important.

When you have a budget in place, you can easily calculate how much money you'd need to cover your basic, no-frills living expenses if you had a sudden loss of income. Write down your goal for your emergency fund and decide on an amount to contribute to it each month, using the "pay yourself first" rule. Keep the fund in a separate account, such as a money market account (not a money market *fund*, which is not FDIC-insured), so you're less tempted to dip into it for nonemergencies. Since emergency funds might be needed without notice, they should be kept in liquid accounts that are easy to cash in quickly.

THE FUN OF FRUGALITY

Don't be discouraged if you feel like you have no extra money to put away. By developing a realistic budget and setting spending and saving goals—and sticking to them—you can create money for savings, even if it's a very small amount to start with.

Decide on a percentage of your income to designate as savings. Financial planners suggest 10 percent, but if 5 or 2 percent is all you can handle at the time, start with that. Don't make the mistake of thinking that if you can't save a large amount of money all at once, it's not worthwhile to try. This couldn't be further from the truth. If you saved $25 a month at 2 percent interest, in five years you'd have $1,578. If you saved $100 a month at 2 percent interest, in five years you'd have $6,312; in ten years you'd have $13,282.

Strategies for Pumping Up Your Savings

Set up a separate savings account. If you mingle your day-to-day funds with your savings, it's almost inevitable that you'll end up using some or all of the savings, and you may never repay them. There's also a mental component. Seeing your savings balance grow from month to month and your financial goals becoming more of a reality is highly motivating.

If you have direct deposit at work and your employer allows you to split your deposit between multiple accounts, consider having a set amount deducted from your paycheck each pay period and deposited in your savings account. It's much easier to save when the money doesn't have to take a detour to your checking account before reaching your savings account. If you don't have this option at work, set up an automatic transfer into your savings account. Online bank accounts will do this for free—they'll even pull money from a different bank. After a while, as you adjust your budget and spending, you won't even miss the money you're putting into savings.

Think of It As a Loan

If you feel forced to dip into your savings in an emergency, consider it a loan. If you can't pay it all back at once, set up a repayment plan and pay yourself as though it were a regular bill. Otherwise you may never replenish your emergency savings.

Use windfalls to pump up your savings instead of spending them. Bonuses, tax refunds, rebates, overtime pay, income from hobbies or yard sales, cash gifts from family, lottery winnings, and other sporadic cash receipts can make faster advances toward your goals without requiring additional spending cutbacks. When you receive a salary increase, put all or part of it into savings each pay period and continue living on your previous salary. When you pay off a loan, continue putting the payment amount aside each month, but pay it into your savings account instead of to the bank or finance company. Because you're already in the habit of doing without that money, you won't even miss it.

Don't Be a Victim of Advertising

With a spending plan, you don't need to deprive yourself of things you really want, but you should question whether you really do want them. Experts recommend these strategies:

- Don't use shopping as a form of recreation.
- Don't shop on impulse.

- For items you really do need or want, look for sales and special offers.
- Shop at outlet or discount stores and websites.
- Before buying appliances, electronics, computer equipment, and other expensive items, research them in *Consumer Reports* or other magazines that do consumer reviews.
- Do some of your shopping at a warehouse club if there's one near you.

Product Reviews

You can find product reviews and cost comparisons online—just be sure the source is reliable and impartial. One good site is www.consumerworld.org, with product reviews, price comparisons, airfare and travel deals, and lots of other consumer resources.

Avoid the Holiday Hangover

If you're like most people, you tend to go overboard on holiday spending, but you can avoid overspending on gifts by setting spending limits. Using your budget, figure out how much you can realistically afford to spend on gifts without going into debt. Make a list of all the people you'd like to buy gifts for, including small gifts for babysitters, teachers, newspaper carriers, and so on. Set a limit for each person on your list, then add up all the amounts and make sure they don't exceed your overall spending limit. Try to allow a cushion for unexpected items or price fluctuations.

PUMPING UP YOUR SAVINGS

Finding the Fat

You may think there's no fat in your budget, but nearly everyone can find some if they look hard enough. Consider it a challenge to find ways to cut your expenses, or make a game of it. By cutting the cable cord and using one or two streaming platforms, you'll have plenty of content at a much lower cost. Think about downsizing your car; less expensive cars usually cost less to repair, maintain, and insure, and may even save you on gas.

Consider buying used instead of new, especially if you're starting a new interest. Check places like *Craigslist*, *Letgo*, and *Facebook Marketplace* for things such as exercise equipment, vehicles, musical instruments, electronics, and more.

SAVING FOR LARGE PURCHASES

Basically, you have a choice: You can either make monthly payments to yourself (and possibly *earn* interest) before you buy, or you can make monthly payments with interest to someone else after you buy. Plus, delaying a larger purchase until you can afford it gives you plenty of time to change your mind about whether it's something you really need or want. If you run right out and charge the item to your credit card or take out a loan, you'll be stuck paying for the item for a long time, and you'll end up paying a lot more for it because of the interest charges.

WHAT KIND OF BANK DO YOU NEED?

Knowing Who's Got Your Money

You probably have a checking account and maybe a savings account, but chances are you don't give much thought to the impact banking has on your finances. Being knowledgeable about how banks work can save you money. You might be surprised just how much your banking arrangements and habits are costing you.

CHOOSING A BANK OR CREDIT UNION

Choosing a bank can have a bigger impact on your finances than you might realize. Important factors to consider include convenience, free ATM access, online banking platform, and fees (which can add up quickly and drain your account). Many banks charge monthly fees unless you maintain a minimum balance or use direct deposit for paychecks. They may also charge your account if you use a live teller (instead of an app or ATM) or a "foreign" (meaning not in their network) bank's ATM. Virtually all financial institutions charge for bouncing checks (that you write or deposit), stopping payment on a check, and overdrawing your account.

Think about your banking habits and what you want your bank to do for you. Identify the services that are most important to you, compare fees for those services between several different banks, and then choose the bank that fits your needs for the best price. If you use an ATM to withdraw cash from your account on a weekly basis, for example, you wouldn't want to choose a bank that doesn't have ATMs near your home or workplace or one that charges a hefty fee for ATM transactions. You may decide to use a traditional brick-and-mortar bank in your neighborhood or a strictly online bank.

Another big choice is deciding between a credit union and a traditional bank. Banks are owned by investors; credit unions are owned and controlled by customers, who are members. Credit unions are nonprofit organizations and return surplus earnings to members in the form of lower interest rates on loans, increasing interest rates on deposits, or offering free or low-cost services. While banks, especially large national banks, may prioritize profits and shareholders, credit unions prioritize their member-customers.

Both banks and credit unions offer accounts that are insured and fully backed by the US government. This ensures that your accounts will be protected for up to $250,000 in each participating financial institution. Banks are backed by the Federal Deposit Insurance Corporation (FDIC); credit unions are covered by the National Credit Union Administration (NCUA).

Joint accounts (accounts with two owners) have $500,000 of protection ($250,000 for each owner) and are treated as separate from any accounts held by each individual owner in his or her own name. That means you would be insured for up to $250,000 in accounts in just your name, as well as half of a $500,000 joint account. Retirement accounts such as IRAs are also treated separately for purposes of the $250,000 FDIC protection. For example, a married couple could have the following accounts FDIC-protected at the same bank:

1. $250,000 in husband's name
2. $250,000 in wife's name
3. $500,000 in a joint account between husband and wife
4. $250,000 in an IRA for the husband
5. $250,000 in an IRA for the wife

That would protect a total of $1,500,000 in one financial institution!

Make Sure Your Bank Is Insured

How do you make sure a bank or credit union is government-insured? The vast majority are, but some are not, so it pays to check. Go to the FDIC website at www.fdic.gov, click on "BankFind" and enter the bank name and state or its URL. For credit unions, visit www.ncua.gov or www.mycreditunion.gov.

ONLINE BANKING

Online banking allows you to manage your money via the Internet—when and where you want. You can view all your banking transactions, move money, view and print your canceled checks, and pay bills online. You can also set up notifications for when checks clear or your balance goes under a predetermined minimum. Many online-only savings accounts offer higher interest rates than traditional banks.

The main benefit of online banking is convenience. You can access your accounts and complete transactions from anywhere at any time. You can automate transactions to beef up your savings or make sure bills get paid on time every month.

Banking Apps

Mobile banking apps add even more convenience than online banking. With these apps, which are offered by many banks and credit unions, you can manage your money from your smartphone, no matter where you are.

These apps allow you to deposit checks remotely, so you don't need to go to the bank or ATM. You can do virtually any banking function using your mobile banking app, including:

- Making transfers
- Paying bills
- Checking your balance
- Reviewing transactions
- Reporting fraud

The only thing these apps can't do? Give you cash. However, they can direct you to the nearest ATM or brick-and-mortar bank so you can get the cash you need quickly.

In addition, payment apps like PayPal, Zelle, and Venmo let you quickly and easily transfer money to other people. You can use these apps for everything from secure online shopping to splitting a dinner check when you're out with friends to sending and receiving money immediately. You can link these apps to bank accounts and credit card accounts, then pay whichever way works better for you at the time.

BANKING PROTECTION

Keeping Your Money Safe

Banking online is actually safer than traditional methods of banking. There are fewer errors when you use technology, and there is less fraud—as long as you're extremely cautious with your login credentials and passwords and never use public Wi-Fi to access personal financial accounts. In addition, every transaction can be tracked in detail.

Staying safe online calls for vigilance, because scammers come up with new ways to separate you from your money every day. Anything that looks fishy probably is; however, you can keep yourself from becoming a victim by keeping an eye out for the most common scams, such as phishing. This happens when you receive an email from what looks like your bank asking you to update your account information. You'll be directed to a website, which will ask you for your personal information, bank account numbers, usernames, and passwords. But the site you go to is not really run by your bank, even if it looks just like your bank's website. Your bank will never ask you for personal financial information in an email, so if you get one like this, delete it without clicking on any of the contents.

Other attacks involve stealing your information from your devices. Software programs may track your communication or keystrokes on your computer, and send that information off to a scammer. Fake outlets can steal information from your phone or tablet when you plug in to recharge. Hackers can get into your devices over public Wi-Fi. Use antivirus and firewall software on your computer, and keep other software (browsers, operating system, etc.) up-to-date. Make sure your phone and tablet have the latest security updates as well. Use two-step authentication whenever possible.

Finally, keep a close watch on your financial accounts (bank, investment, and retirement) and keep a tight lid on your banking information. Simply telling somebody your account number can expose you to problems, so don't divulge your banking information over the phone or via the web unless you know whom you're dealing with. If you suspect that somebody else is using your account, call your bank immediately.

With the Help of Software

Quicken and Mint are two popular apps that let you use online banking information to further your financial plans. Both are robust personal finance programs that allow you to download your banking transactions and help to manage your finances and budget, balance your checkbook, pay bills electronically, prepare and file your taxes, track investments, and build a financial plan for your future.

Watch Out for Electronic Spying

Beware of skimming devices posing as ATMs. They record electronically stored information from the magnetic stripe of your card or your personal identification number (PIN) as you enter it. The thieves then skim money from your bank account. Stick to bank ATMs instead of those in malls, airports, and other public places.

OVERDRAFT PROTECTION

Overdraft protection is a checking account feature that makes sure checks, ATM withdrawals, and debit card transactions that would send your account balance below zero still get covered in full and helps you avoid overdraft fees (which can be as high as $34 per incident). It provides a safety net to protect you from accidentally overdrawing your account, but that protection comes at a price; on average, overdraft protection fees run around $12. That may sound like a good deal, but it's not; it's just the start of overdraft-related fees.

Some banks allow you to cover overdrafts automatically from your savings account or with a bank credit card. The most common method of covering overdrafts involves establishing a line of credit, which typically has an interest rate that can be as much as two times higher than the going rates on credit cards or loans. The cost to you could be substantial if you don't repay it right away.

If your overdraft protection is linked to your credit card, the bank issues a cash advance to cover your overdraft and charges it to your credit card. You pay a cash advance fee of 2 to 3 percent plus the fee your bank charges for the transaction, plus whatever interest you incur before you pay the cash advance back.

Your best bet is to be your own overdraft protection. Pay close attention to the balance in your checking account, especially if you regularly use your debit card or payment apps like Zelle or Venmo that are linked to your checking account. Set up account balance alerts that let you know when you're running low on funds. If you know you're having trouble covering all of your expenses, revisit your budget and make some changes; that will help keep you from drowning in bank fees that you really can't afford.

BEWARE OUT-OF-NETWORK FEES

When you use an ATM that is not owned by your bank or in its network, your bank will charge you an out-of-network fee. On top of that, you may incur a surcharge from the foreign ATM provider, which gets charged in addition to fees charged by your own bank.

Here's an example of how it works: You withdraw $20 from an ATM that doesn't belong to your bank, and that ATM charges a $1.50 fee. Your bank then adds an out-of-network surcharge of $3.00. You've just paid $4.50 in service fees, 22.5 percent of your withdrawal amount, to access $20 of your own money.

You can minimize ATM fees by:

- Establishing an account at a bank with a large ATM network so you don't get stuck using out-of-network ATMs.
- Planning cash withdrawals when you can access your own bank's ATMs, or look for ATMs that don't impose a surcharge (which will be indicated on the ATM).
- Withdrawing large amounts of cash less often rather than smaller amounts more often.
- Using mobile banking apps to pay for purchases or to transfer money to other people.
- Avoiding higher-cost ATMs found in convenience stores, hotels, casinos, restaurants, and airports.

DEBIT CARDS

Most ATM cards also function as debit cards. Debit cards work similarly to credit cards, but the money is taken directly from the connected bank account rather than being added to your credit card bill. You can only pay with the debit card if you have enough cash in your account to cover the purchase, or you may overdraw your account or need expensive overdraft protection to kick in.

Two Ways Debit Cards Work

When you're using your debit card for purchases, you may have a choice of using it as a credit card. The main difference in this situation is whether or not you'll have to enter your PIN when you check out. If you use it as a debit card, you may be able to get additional cash back with your purchase. Don't be confused by the Visa or Mastercard logo on your debit card; it is not a credit card. No matter which way you use this card, the money will come straight out of your bank account immediately.

Debit Card Safety

Debit card fraud can be harder to recover from than credit card fraud. After all, cash gets immediately taken from your account with a debit card, meaning you've already lost money by the time you notice fraud. If you don't act quickly, it may be harder to recover the full amount stolen. That's why it's crucial to monitor your bank accounts and make sure all the transactions are yours.

If your debit card is lost or stolen, reporting it within two business days will limit your losses to $50 by law (though some banks may refund the full amount of the fraudulent charge). Waiting longer than that can bump your potential losses up to $500. If your card isn't missing, you have sixty days from the day your bank statement was sent or posted online to report fraudulent transactions for full protection.

How can someone use your debit card if you still have it? Thieves may attach skimmers (sort of like data recording devices) to ATMs to capture your debit card information, then use it to make purchases. Nonsecure websites, those with addresses that start with *http* rather than *https*, make it easier for unscrupulous people to steal your debit card data.

To keep your debit card as secure as possible:

- Stick with bank ATMs, as their constant surveillance may better deter skimmers
- Change your PIN regularly and keep it protected by never writing the number down
- Use your debit card as a credit card when shopping to avoid entering your PIN in public
- Never use your debit card online with public Wi-Fi
- Pay attention to your bank statements and current transactions
- Report anything suspicious immediately

Taking these steps will help keep your debit card more secure and protect your bank account from fraudulent withdrawals.

WHERE TO STASH YOUR CASH

Keeping It Available

What do you do with money that you want to be able to access quickly when needed, such as your emergency fund? If you put it in a CD (certificate of deposit), you may incur penalties if you have to withdraw it before the lock-in term expires. If you mingle it with your checking account, you're more likely to dip into it. Your savings account may not earn a very high interest rate. Under your mattress or in your cookie jar are really not viable options. So where is the best place to stash your cash?

CHECKING AND SAVINGS ACCOUNTS

Savings often end up sitting in the checking account just because it's the easiest option. It's not a good idea, though. Savings should be segregated from your day-to-day spending money for several reasons, including the fact that it's much too easy to dip into your savings if that money is mingled with your checking account. In most cases, you'll also earn more interest in a nonchecking account. Savings accounts usually pay higher interest rates than checking accounts because the money is expected to sit there longer. Savings accounts, especially higher-interest online savings accounts, are a good place to park your emergency savings because you'll have instant access to your cash when you need it. Because savings-account interest rates usually don't keep up with the rate of inflation, it's best not to store more money than you need to cover three to six months' worth of living expenses there.

Internet Bank Accounts

If you want to try for a higher interest rate, look at online bank accounts. One of the most attractive features of these accounts is the higher interest rate they pay on deposits, plus they often have no minimum balance requirements. Keep in mind that it can take up to three business days to transfer money from your online savings account into your checking account. You may be able to get immediate cash if the account comes with an ATM/debit card. Be aware that you're only allowed to make six withdrawals per month from online savings accounts.

Money Market Deposit Accounts

Money market deposit accounts, as opposed to money market funds, are also FDIC-insured. They usually require a minimum balance of $1,000 or more—sometimes as much as $10,000 or $25,000—but they pay higher interest rates than traditional savings accounts. If your account balance falls below the minimum, you'll probably be charged an account maintenance fee, which usually wipes out any gains from the higher interest rate. These accounts also limit withdrawals to six per month.

Certificates of Deposit

CDs are like locked-in savings accounts. You agree to leave your money in the bank for an agreed-upon term (usually three months to five years) in return for a higher guaranteed interest rate on your principal. Most of the time (but not always), longer terms come with higher interest rates. Some CDs come with step-up rates where your interest rate increases at specific intervals. If you withdraw all or part of your CD funds before the maturity date, the bank will charge a penalty.

BANKING COSTS

Sometimes you can gain as much by cutting insignificant costs that add up over time as you can by earning additional income. Banking costs are a good example. Banks charge so many different types of fees, that you may not realize what your real costs are. With minimum balance requirements, ATM fees, and overdraft charges, even your basic checking and savings accounts might be costing you more than they should. In addition, if your money could be earning more interest somewhere else, you've lost an opportunity. For example, keeping a low-interest savings account in a traditional bank rather than moving it to a higher-interest online savings account costs you the extra interest you would have earned.

Service versus Cost

Be aware of your banking costs and make intelligent trade-offs to get the services you use for the lowest overall cost. If keeping a minimum balance in your checking account costs you $5 a month in opportunity costs but saves you $7 in fees, it makes sense to go with that option. If you have savings and checking accounts at the same bank, keep only as much money in the checking account as you need to pay bills that are due immediately. Let the rest of your funds go to work for you by earning interest in your savings account. When interest rates are very low, the earnings may be minimal, but you'll still earn more than zero.

Minimizing Fees

Most banks charge a long menu of fees for consumer checking accounts, and those fees can add up very quickly. What's worse, when you aren't expecting them, bank fees can even end up triggering more bank fees. You can eliminate a lot of these budget-busting fees by taking simple actions.

- *Monthly maintenance fees*. Many banks charge maintenance fees of $10 to $12 per month if your balance dips below a preset minimum. You can avoid those fees by making sure you keep that minimum cushion in your account at all times, having the bank waive the fee by setting up direct deposits for your paychecks, or switching to a no-monthly-fee checking account.

- *Overdraft fees*. When your checking account goes into a negative balance, you'll be charged overdraft fees, and these can run more than $30 *each*. Make sure you account for everything that drains your account, including automatic payments, ordering checks, ATM withdrawals, debit card transactions, and bank fees.

- *ATM fees*. Find out if your bank charges for "foreign" ATM transactions (meaning you used a different institution's ATM, like at another bank or a convenience store). Those fees can range from $2 to $10 every time you use that foreign ATM. If your bank charges for this, make it a point to only use your bank's ATM, and take out enough cash to last until the next time you swing by.

- *Returned-item fees*. If you deposit a check that bounces (meaning the person who paid you didn't have enough money in his or her account to cover the payment), your bank will probably charge you a fee, sometimes as much as $15. Not only will that deposit not be in your account; you'll also be out the amount of the fee.

- *Paper statement fees*. Some banks now charge fees—up to $2 a month!—for mailing out paper statements. Switching to online statements will kill that fee and save some trees.

Bottom line: Banks charge fees for pretty much everything. Go to your bank's website and take a look at the schedule of fees so you know exactly what the institution is charging you for.

Excellent websites to compare all types of bank rates include www.bankrate.com and www.nerdwallet.com.

Chapter 3

Managing Credit Cards

Using credit cards can make your life easier, but they can also trap you in high-interest debt. Running a balance on your credit cards can set back your financial goals and even keep you from reaching them. To avoid this, it's important to understand how credit cards really work and how you can make them work in your favor.

CREDIT CARDS

The Good, the Bad, and the Ugly

When you pay by credit card, it doesn't feel like you're spending money. In fact, you're not really spending money—you're borrowing money. You know that you'll have to pay the bill eventually, but the promise of small minimum payments can make purchases seem like bargains. Credit card companies are well aware of this psychological disconnect, and they take full advantage of it. That's how so many people end up with overwhelming credit card debt. But if you know how they work before you start using them, you can turn credit cards into tools that help you build up a credit history and improve your financial situation, rather than the other way around.

On the plus side, using a credit card responsibly and mindfully can help you to establish good credit so when it's time to buy a house or a new car you qualify for the best possible terms and lowest interest rates on the mortgage or car loan. Your card may also give back rewards, which can be valuable as long as you pay off the card every month. Most credit cards also offer purchase protection and other benefits. But the same cards that provide great convenience may become the means by which you end up thousands of dollars in debt, as purchases you make become much more expensive because of high interest rates.

THE FALSE APPEAL OF CREDIT

The message of credit cards is one of instant gratification—you can have it all now. Credit card companies increase convenience at every turn. Their goal is getting you to use your credit card for everything and make the smallest possible monthly payments. They encourage you to overspend by dangling rewards in front of you. They discourage you from paying your balance in full by offering the option of minimum payments, which seem like monthly payments but aren't. Credit card companies like it when you pay late (as long as you do pay), so they can increase your APR (annual percentage rate) and charge you penalties. After all, the more money you owe and the longer you owe it, the more money they make. And they're in this to make as much money off of you as possible.

WHAT'S OUT THERE

When it comes to getting credit cards, you have hundreds of choices. Major credit card issuers include Visa, Mastercard, and American Express. These card companies allow you to make purchases up to a preset credit limit ranging from $500 to $10,000 or more, depending on your income and credit history. You can pay the balance in full each month, the minimum required by the card company (typically around 2 to 4 percent of the balance), or any amount in between.

What Are Gold and Platinum Cards?

These are cards that include extra perks such as collision coverage when you rent a car, extended warranties on certain items, travel insurance, special discounts, and other exclusive benefits. They sound appealing, but you have to consider exactly what you get for the privilege of paying a much higher annual fee.

In-house credit cards, also called store cards, allow you to charge purchases at a particular chain of retailers, such as department stores and gas stations, and make monthly payments, including interest charges. Many retailers do offer certain advantages to their cardholders, such as additional discounts on their merchandise and exclusive shopping opportunities, particularly around the holidays.

The Cost of Credit

There are several types of costs associated with credit cards. The annual fee is a flat dollar amount the issuer charges each year for the use of the card. Many, but not all, issuers charge annual fees. Finance charges are calculated based on the interest rate your card issuer charges and are the main cost of using credit. These rates vary significantly from one card to another, so you can save a lot of money by shopping around for a card with a lower interest rate. Other fees that you might incur on your credit card include application fees, processing fees, charges for exceeding your credit limit, late-payment fees, balance-transfer fees, and fees on cash advances.

Grace Periods

The grace period, commonly twenty-five days, is the time between the date you're billed and the date your payment is due. If you pay your entire balance within the grace period, you may not incur any interest charges. If you carry a balance, there's often no grace period on new purchases, so interest starts accruing from the date of purchase. Some issuers charge interest from the day you make the purchase, even if you pay your balance in full, so in effect there is no grace period. When you add the fact that charges made at the start of the monthly billing cycle already give you a one-month deferral on payment, this grace period may result in a six-week, interest-free deferral on payment. The Credit CARD Act of 2009 mandates that the grace period, if offered, shall be for a minimum of twenty-one days.

CHOOSING WHAT'S BEST FOR YOU

Before you choose a credit card, think about how you intend to use it. If you pay the balance in full every month, the annual fee and other charges may be more important than the APR (the interest rate charged), so you should look for a no-fee or low-fee card. Even if the issuer charges an annual fee, you may be able to get it waived by calling and asking the company to remove it. If you carry a balance and pay for your purchases over time, the APR and the method of computing your balance are most important, so you'll want to look for the lowest interest rate and the longest grace period.

Beware of teaser rates, which sound tempting because the introductory rate is much lower than the going rate on most cards. The downside is that if you have a balance on the card when the introductory rate ends, you could be in worse shape than if you'd had a higher rate all along, depending on how high the rate spikes at the end of the introductory offer and whether interest accrues all the way back to the original purchase date. It is also imperative that you make all minimum payments during the introductory period in a timely manner, or the rate will revert instantly to that higher rate.

PAY THEM OFF!

Keeping Your Balance Down

The credit card company's goal is to make as much money as possible from your account. When they establish a low minimum monthly payment, they're not trying to do you a favor; they're trying to maximize their profits by keeping you in debt for a long time.

DON'T PAY THE MINIMUM

By paying credit card interest of $50 a month you've lost the opportunity to invest that money: Invested at 6 percent, $50 a month would total more than $57,000 in thirty-two years, the time it would take you to pay off a $2,500 balance at an APR of 19 percent (the average new credit card rate in 2020) if you never use the credit card again and make only the minimum payment. Plus, in that time you would pay more than $7,300 in interest charges.

Most credit card companies calculate minimum monthly payments at 1 or 2 percent of the balance due, including interest. If you made a purchase of $2,500 at an annual interest rate of 18 percent, it would take you more than twenty-seven years to pay off the balance by making only the minimum monthly payment. Here's how that works: Initially, 2 percent of your balance would give you a minimum payment of $50, with around 75 percent, or $37.50 ($2,500 × 18 percent ÷ 12), going toward interest, and only 25 percent, or $12.50, reducing the amount you borrowed.

By the time you paid off the $2,500, you would have ended up paying interest of $5,897 in addition to the $2,500 principal you borrowed. Your $2,500 item will have cost you $8,397. How can you ever get ahead financially if you're paying such exorbitant prices?

Paying any amount more than the minimum payment—even just $5 extra—can shave years and thousands of dollars from that payoff. Whenever possible, try not to use credit cards for purchases you can't afford to pay in full right away.

PROTECTING YOURSELF AGAINST LOSSES

It's getting more and more difficult to protect your credit cards from theft. Thieves and scam artists keep coming up with more clever ruses to obtain the information they need to use your cards fraudulently or obtain credit in your name. Even your identity can be stolen.

Keep Your Credit Cards Safe

Your best protection against credit card fraud is to know where your cards are at all times. Don't carry credit cards with you unless you know you're going to need them. Don't leave them lying around on your desk at work or in your car or anywhere else they could be accessible to others. When you get a renewal credit card or you cancel a card, cut the old card up into small pieces, being sure to cut through the number. Ideally, run old cards through the shredder.

Don't disclose your credit card number over the phone unless you're dealing with a reputable company and you're the one who placed the call to them. Scammers often use phishing scams whereby a computer dialer poses as your bank and asks you to call in to discuss transactions in your account. They send emails that look like they're from your credit card company, warning you about fraudulent charges and asking you to enter your login information to verify your identity. Your bank will never ask you for personal information by email.

If Your Card Is Lost or Stolen

As soon as you realize your credit card, ATM card, or debit card has been lost or stolen, report the loss immediately to the bank or other issuer in order to limit your liability if the card is used fraudulently. Keep a list of your credit card numbers in a safe place so you can report the loss as quickly as possible.

Under federal law, if you report the loss before any unauthorized charges are made to your credit card, you can't be held responsible for any charges. If a thief uses your card before you report it missing, the most you will owe for unauthorized charges is $50 per card. If somebody uses your credit card number fraudulently without physically stealing the card itself, you are not liable for the charges.

After the loss of your card, review your monthly statements carefully and report in writing any unauthorized charges. Lost credit cards should also be reported to each of the major credit reporting agencies: Experian, TransUnion, and Equifax. Ask them to place a security alert or a freeze on your account to intercept possibly fraudulent applications for credit.

Identity Theft

Identity theft occurs when someone uses your personal information such as your name, credit card number, or Social Security number to commit fraud or theft. Using just your date of birth and Social Security number, thieves can apply for a credit card in your name, and rack up big charges before you even know the account has been opened. When the balance isn't paid, the delinquency is reflected in your credit history.

Some thieves will even call your credit card company and report a change of address on your account, or they'll access your account online and change the password and contact information so you can no longer access your account. Other scams include setting up cellular phone service in your name or opening a bank account in your name.

Be careful of how and where you dispose of bank statements, credit card offers, credit card statements, or any document that includes your date of birth or Social Security number. Consider purchasing a personal shredder and shredding these documents before throwing them in the trash. If you believe you have become a victim of identity theft, file a report with your creditors, the three credit reporting bureaus, the IRS, and your local police as soon as possible.

THE CREDIT CARD ACT OF 2009

Effective February 22, 2010, the Credit Card Accountability Responsibility and Disclosure Act (also called the CARD Act) offers strong protections to credit card holders and limits the credit card issuers' ability to charge credit card holders unfairly. Some highlights of this law are:

- Credit card issuers have to include minimum payment warnings on every bill, including information such as how long it would take to pay off the balance if only minimum payments were made.
- Should you be more than sixty days behind on payments, a retroactive increase in your interest rate will be allowed; however, once you have made timely payments for a six-month period, the issuer must restore your rate.

- If you open a new credit card, there may not be any rate increase for the first twelve months, unless certain situations apply (your card comes with a variable interest rate, for example).
- Card issuers must deny any purchase that would put the cardholder over the limit of the card unless the cardholder agrees to pay the over-the-limit fee.
- Total fees charged on a credit card for the first twelve months cannot exceed 25 percent of the card's initial limit (also called credit line).
- Statements must be mailed or delivered at least twenty-one days prior to the due date.
- Credit card issuers may not assess interest charges on balances from previous billing cycles or balances that were already paid. This is known as double-cycle billing.
- Monthly due dates must always be on the same day of the month. Any weekend or bank holiday due dates must be extended to the next business day.
- All payments received by 5 p.m. must be recorded as being received on that day.
- Any changes to credit card terms must be accompanied by at least forty-five days' advance notice.

BUILDING AND REPAIRING CREDIT RESPONSIBLY

Using Your Credit Report

Credit is a valuable tool, but as with all tools, you must learn to use it carefully and responsibly. This means, above all, paying close attention to your credit report.

YOUR CREDIT REPORT AND HOW IT WORKS

A credit report is a record of your credit history as reported to credit bureaus by your bank, credit card companies, department stores, and other businesses you've borrowed from. Potential lenders use the information in your credit report to decide whether they want to take the risk of issuing you credit. If you understand how credit reports work, you can protect your rights and avoid being taken advantage of by unscrupulous credit repair clinics and so-called credit doctors.

Your Rights about Credit

Under the Fair Credit Reporting Act, you have specific rights related to your credit report. You can read about these rights on the Federal Trade Commission's (FTC) website at www.ftc.gov.

If you're thinking about buying a house or applying for credit for any other big purchase, you'll need a good credit report. It's always best to know what's on it before your lender does, so you'll have an opportunity to clean up any discrepancies or errors.

What's in a Credit Report?

Your credit report includes the following basic personal information:

- Name
- Current and previous addresses
- Telephone number
- Social Security number
- Date of birth
- Current and previous employers

The credit history section includes information about each credit account, including the date opened, credit limit or loan amount, balance, monthly payment, and your payment pattern during the past several years. Bankruptcies, accounts sent to collection agencies, unpaid child support or alimony, tax liens, car repossessions, court records of tax liens and monetary judgments, and the names of businesses or individuals who have obtained a copy of your credit report are also included. In addition, your report contains information obtained from public records, such as your job history, whether you own your home, and whether you've filed for bankruptcy. When issues between you and a creditor can't be resolved, the comments and explanations you're allowed to add to your credit report and the creditor's response to your statements become part of your credit report. If an account was turned over to a collection agency, your report will include it as a "collection account" until it's paid in full; then it will be noted as a "paid collection" and will stay on your credit report for seven years from the date of the first missed payment.

Review Your Credit Report

Financial advisors recommend that you obtain a copy of your credit report at least once a year and review it carefully. The Fair Credit Reporting Act allows you to get one free credit report from each credit reporting company every year. If you've been turned down for credit, housing, or employment because of information in your report, you may be entitled to an additional free copy of your credit report. Some states require that credit bureaus provide free copies or charge a reduced price for residents of that state, so you may find a variety of ways to get more than one free credit report per year from each of the credit reporting companies.

As mentioned previously, there are three main credit bureaus: Equifax, Experian, and TransUnion. Because some creditors report to only one of the bureaus, the information in your credit report may differ somewhat from one bureau to the other; experts recommend that you obtain a copy of your report from each of the three major credit bureaus once a year.

To order your credit reports use the official site created by the three major credit reporting companies: www.annualcreditreport .com. If you use a different site, it's likely that you won't get your credit reports for free. Many imposter sites claim to offer free reports and credit scores, but they will want a fee from you sooner or later, or they might just be phishing for your personal information.

If you find an error in your credit report, send a letter to the credit bureau explaining the error in as much detail as possible. You can find sample letters on the Consumer Financial Protection Bureau

(CFPB) website at www.consumerfinance.gov. Provide any documents that help prove your statements. Send everything certified mail, return receipt requested. If you don't get an answer within forty days or so, follow up with them.

What's Not in Your Credit Report

Your credit report does not include information about your race or national origin, religion, personal lifestyle, political affiliation, medical history, criminal record, or other information unrelated to your credit history and ability to repay debt.

How Do Lenders Use the Credit Report?

Lenders use the information in your credit report to evaluate your debt capacity, your collateral, your capital, and your expected ability to repay the debt. Their evaluation of your payment probability is partly based on the stability of your employment and residency history. To evaluate your debt capacity, lenders look at your open credit limits, current debts, and other payments to get a sense of how much debt you can afford based on your income and credit burden. They're more likely to extend you credit that's secured by collateral. For example, the car you purchase is the collateral for your car loan. If you default on the loan, the car can be repossessed, so there's less risk to the lender. Down payments also work in your favor, as the lender can see that you have planned for and invested in the purchase.

Increasingly, lenders have been making their lending decisions by focusing on your credit score, which is a number indicating how likely you are to make payments on time and repay loans. The score is computer-generated and largely based on your use of credit in the past— how long you've used credit, how much you use, and how responsibly you've used it. All in all, they may look at your income, education, job stability, how often you've moved, whether you own your own home, how often you take out cash advances, how close you are to your credit limits, how many credit cards you have, and past payment history. A computer compares this information to patterns from thousands of other consumers and predicts your level of credit risk.

Many banks and credit card issuers offer free credit score tracking as part of their service; you can find the score on your monthly statement or by going online and logging in to your account. Many websites also offer free credit score tracking, but you need to watch out for scam artists who are just trying to collect your personal information. Reliable sites for this include *Credit Karma*, *Credit Sesame*, and *NerdWallet*. Many money management apps (like Mint) also keep track of your credit score. While there are several different credit scoring models out there, the FICO (Fair Isaac Corporation) credit score is most often used by lenders and others. All three major credit bureaus offer this option with your credit report or as a separate option.

Keeping track of your credit score can motivate you to improve it. Some of the best ways to improve your credit include paying every bill on time every month, keeping credit card balances below 30 percent of your available credit, avoiding the closure of unused credit cards and the opening of new credit cards, and checking your credit report for any inaccuracies.

MAKE A PAYDOWN PLAN

When you're ready to start paying down your debt, make a plan that you can stick to. The best plans involve focusing on one debt at a time (your "focus" debt). When you zero in on a single debt, it's easier to make and see progress. Plus, it's much less stressful to face a mole-hill than a mountain.

The two most popular paydown plans are the snowball method and the avalanche method. Either will help you dig your way out of debt, so choose whichever feels more comfortable for you. Avalanche normally works a little bit faster and saves you a little more interest. But it's usually easier for people to stick with the snowball method because there are more victories early on.

Both methods work well, and you don't have to lock yourself in; you can switch between them whenever you want. The trick for success here is to pick the one you think will be easier to start with, and then get started.

No Matter Which Plan You Choose...

Whichever method you go for, make sure to do these four things:

1. Pick one focus debt that you'll put extra money toward
2. Throw every dollar you can at that focus debt
3. Make multiple payments throughout the month (rather than one on the due date) to minimize the next month's interest charge
4. Make on-time minimum payments every month on every debt

That last point is important. Any skipped or late payments will be hit with expensive penalties that take your debt in the wrong direction and make it even harder to pay down. Avoid even the possibility of late payments by setting up automatic payments to cover the minimum for every credit card, including the focus debt.

There is a fifth thing to do, but this one can be extra tough: Stop using your credit cards except for actual emergencies. It's practically impossible to pay credit card debt off if you're adding new charges every month.

The Avalanche Method

With the avalanche method, you'll rank your credit card debts by interest rate, from highest to lowest, and focus on the most expensive debt first. Regardless of how big that debt is, you'll save money in interest, which leaves more money for paying down the balance.

You can find your current credit card interest rates (sometimes listed as APR) right on the statements. Pick the card with the highest rate, and start paying that one down as fast as you can. Once it's paid off, you'll move to the next highest rate, and keep going until all the cards are paid off.

The Snowball Method

If you like extra encouragement and motivation, the snowball method may work well for you. Using this plan, you'll pay down your first focus debt more quickly, and get a sense of accomplishment as you cross it off the list. You'll be able to clearly see your progress, and that little rush (it's true; it's science) will help keep the paydown practice going.

With this method, you'll list your debt in order of balance, from lowest to highest. Your smallest debt will be your first focus debt. Once that one's settled, you'll use the money you'd been putting toward it to pay the next debt on your list (your payments will "snowball"). You'll keep paying off debts and moving down the list until all the debts are paid off.

BORROWING FROM YOUR 401(K)

Most 401(k) plans include a loan feature that allows you to borrow money from your retirement account and repay it in five years or less at an interest rate determined by your plan administrator, usually a couple of points above the prime rate. Each plan can set its own limits on the amount you can borrow, but most follow IRS guidelines. Under the CARES Act of 2020, you can borrow up to $100,000 from your 401(k) account. Plus, the CARES Act also extends the payback period: Any loan payments that would be due by December 31, 2020, can be delayed for up to one year (interest will still accrue and increase the loan balance during that time). Though this might seem like a good source of funds to use for everyday expenses or to pay down your debt, it comes with some significant drawbacks.

Your 401(k) and Debt

Using your 401(k) to pay off debts can threaten your financial future. Your 401(k) is there to support you during retirement. If you start pulling out that money now, you will end up with less money in retirement, when it's harder to borrow, cut costs, and find work.

Paying Yourself Back

Taking money out of your 401(k) account could have a significant impact on your retirement income even if you pay the money back. That's because you have less money invested to earn interest, dividends, and capital gains. Also, many employers won't allow contributions while there's a loan outstanding. Even if your loan is repaid in one year with interest, going that long without making new contributions will have a long-term impact on how much you accumulate by the time you reach retirement age.

The Danger of Job Loss

Perhaps even worse than reducing the potential accumulation of earnings is the danger of being stuck with a loan balance if your employment terminates, whether it's because you've accepted a job elsewhere or you were fired or laid off. If you have an outstanding loan at the time your employment ends, you'll have to pay it back in full by the due date of your next tax return. If you don't, the loan will count as an early withdrawal, subject to income taxes and a 10 percent early withdrawal penalty.

Let's say you borrowed $12,000 and repaid $2,000 before changing jobs. Your loan balance at termination is $10,000. If you can't come up with the money to repay it by the due date of your next tax return, it will be considered a premature withdrawal. If you're in the 22 percent tax bracket, you'll have to pay $2,200 in income taxes, plus another $1,000 (10 percent) early withdrawal penalty. All of a sudden your low-interest loan doesn't look so good. On top of that, if you have no other way to come up with the money to pay the taxes and you have to take them from your 401(k) plan too, that money will also be subject to taxes and penalties. Either action could decimate the retirement fund that you've worked so hard to build.

CREDIT COUNSELING SERVICE

If you start searching for help in your struggle to get out of debt, you'll find a lot of websites offering credit counseling and loan consolidations, but not all of them will be working in your best interests. The right professionals will help you improve your money management skills. They'll come up with realistic, workable solutions for paying off your debt and will give you solid guidance on other financial matters (like improving your credit score). Anyone who asks you to just turn everything over to them, promises to "fix" your situation, or seems uninterested in helping you figure out how to manage your financial situation is not the right help.

If dealing with your debt is more than you can handle on your own, consider working with a credit counselor. Reputable credit counselors will help you create a realistic debt repayment plan and show you ways to avoid taking on any new debt. They work with you to come up with an amount you can realistically afford to pay each month. They will talk with your creditors and get them to accept alternative payment terms that your budget can handle. This often involves extending your loan term, which lowers your monthly payments. Reputable, experienced counselors may be able to help get some of your interest rates (like penalty rates) lowered, get creditors to waive fees, and even put a stop to stressful collection calls.

How to Find a Reputable Credit Counselor

Most trustworthy credit counseling agencies are set up as nonprofits. These companies charge very low (sometimes no) fees to help you rebuild your finances in a more positive way. Look for someone who has a solid reputation and a high success rate for helping people get out of debt.

The best credit counselors are trained and certified and will show you their accreditation. You can find reliable, verified information about any credit counseling agencies you're considering working with from the National Foundation for Credit Counseling (NFCC) at www.nfcc .org or the Financial Counseling Association of America (FCAA) at www.fcaa.org.

REPAIRING DAMAGED CREDIT

Fixing a Problem

Sometimes people make unwise choices or take on more credit than they can handle and end up with a bad credit history. Sometimes they acquire bad credit through divorce, loss of a spouse, or unexpected healthcare costs. If you have poor credit you may still be able to borrow money or qualify for credit cards, but it will come with a higher interest rate, and the terms won't be as favorable as they are for those with good credit.

HOW TO IMPROVE YOUR CREDIT

There are simple steps you can take to improve your credit score, no matter what shape it's in. It won't happen instantly, and it will take some work, but you can do it. In fact, if you take these actions and stick with them, you may be able to bump your score up by 100 points in just a couple of months (maybe even faster).

You can boost your credit score and keep it up by doing these things:

- Review your credit report right now and at least once a year. Clearing up mistakes (and there will probably be at least one) can help your score.
- Pay every bill on time every month. Get current with all of your bills, and stay current. If you can't make a full payment on time, alert your creditor ahead of time, and they'll probably work with you to keep that from affecting your account or your credit score.

- Don't use more than 30 percent of your available credit (also called credit utilization) on revolving debt such as credit cards. If the amount you owe is more than that, work on paying that down more quickly to get it back below the 30 percent mark.
- Don't take on any new debt or apply for any new credit cards. Inquiries and new debt can lower your score.
- Don't cancel any credit cards after you pay them off. Canceling cards reduces your available credit, which has the effect of increasing your credit utilization, and that will knock your score down. Stop using them, but don't cancel them (at least not right away).

Secured Cards

A secured credit card can help you build credit so that you can get credit in the future. A secured credit card works like a regular credit card with a cash safety net. Basically, you supply a cash deposit (the secured part) to cover your credit limit, then use the card and make on-time monthly payments.

Check On Credit Reporting

Since your goal with a secured card is to establish or reestablish good credit, make sure that the company issuing the card reports to a credit bureau. Otherwise, the card can't help you build or repair your credit history.

If you don't pay your bills, the card issuer will use the money from your deposit to cover your debt. It may be difficult to come up with the amount to deposit, but you can build a credit history using this method. Many people find that after twelve to eighteen months of making timely payments on a secured card they can "graduate" to a regular credit card.

Don't Fall for Scams

Don't fall for advice given by some "credit repair services" or "credit doctors" telling you to obtain an Employer Identification Number (EIN). They'll suggest you apply for credit using that instead of your Social Security number, so your credit history doesn't pop up when a credit check is performed. If someone tells you to do that, don't. This is a felony.

Questionable Credit Repair Offers

If you have poor credit, you're more susceptible to questionable credit offers, so stay on your toes. Don't fall for offers of easy ways to repair your credit. You have the legal right to correct any errors in your credit report by directly contacting the credit reporting bureaus; don't pay someone to do this for you. Some credit repair companies make false claims about their ability to clean up your credit. Only the creditor or the credit reporting bureau can remove a debt from your record, and the only way to clean up your credit history is by making payments on time for several years and paying off your debts.

USING CREDIT CARDS WISELY

A Great Tool

Credit cards can be a great tool when used wisely. When you avoid overspending on credit you can begin to use credit cards to your advantage. Use those cards right, and the credit card companies will be paying you to borrow money from them. By paying off your cards in full every month, never running a balance, and taking advantage of rewards, you can actually earn money by using your credit cards.

STAYING OUT OF TROUBLE

What is the key to staying out of credit card debt? Never borrow more than you can afford to pay back right away. Your credit card purchases should fit into your budget. Plan every purchase and know how you'll pay for it before you use your credit card. With a solid spending cap in place, your credit card balance won't grow out of control.

For example, people tend to spend more around the holidays. If you use your credit cards to do holiday shopping, you may not pay off the charges until months later. Make a holiday spending budget before you shop, and if you can, try saving small amounts of money throughout the year in a special holiday gift fund. Using credit cards often leads to impulse spending and overspending, and those items that seemed like such bargains end up costing you 10 to 20 percent more than you thought, due to credit card interest.

Some people use their credit card for nearly all of their expenses and pay off the balance in full at the end of the month. This can help in budgeting and keeping track of where their money goes. If you don't have the money or the discipline to pay off your balance every month, you should avoid using a credit card for things such as clothing, food, gas, dining out, and other recurring expenses.

Avoid Cash Advances

Cash advances on credit cards come with huge price tags, including higher interest rates and fees. Cash advances almost always come with a transaction fee of anywhere between 2 and 3 percent of the amount you get. Plus, grace periods don't apply to cash advances, so you pay interest from the day you get the cash. To add insult to injury, the interest rate on cash advances is significantly higher than the rate on purchases. All in all, your cash advance can end up costing you a bundle of money. Bottom line: Don't use your credit card like a bank account, and avoid cash advances whenever possible.

Cash Advance Fees

Visa card holders take out a staggering $100 billion a year in cash advances. At an average up-front fee of 4–5 percent, cash advances are generating $3 billion a year to Visa in this type of fee alone.

LOWERING YOUR CREDIT CARD RATE

Credit card companies will often lower your interest rate if you simply ask. Call the company and tell them that you've received credit card offers with lower rates and ask if they can lower your rate so you don't have to switch. If you've been a good customer and have been with the company a while, you stand a good chance of getting your rate reduced.

PRIORITIZE YOUR BILLS

Pay Them in Order

Some payments are more important than others. For example, it's important to keep your house, as well as to get to work so that you can earn some money. If your situation is so dire that you can't pay all your bills, prioritize your debts and expenses and pay the most important ones first, in this order:

- Mortgage or rent
- Utilities (including phone and Internet)
- Car loan and auto insurance
- Other insurance (homeowners, health)
- Loans (secured loans, student loans, finance companies)
- Credit cards
- Miscellaneous

Talk to the creditors you can't pay fully and let them know you intend to meet your obligations but need some time. They may be willing to give you a month or two and tack the payments on to the end of your loan, reduce your interest rate, or re-age your account so it's not reported as delinquent to the credit bureaus.

Chapter 4

Understanding Loans

Understanding different types of debt can help you choose the kind of loan that makes the most sense for you. It can also make you less susceptible to being taken advantage of, and may help you avoid bankruptcy.

INSTALLMENT, SECURED, AND UNSECURED LOANS

Borrowing Money

All loans are alike in some ways. You borrow an amount of money, called the *principal*, for a set amount of time, called the *term*, at a fixed or variable interest rate. Most loans are installment loans, which require regular payments, usually every month, until the full loan is paid back with interest. Some loans require the principal to be repaid all at once.

Secured and Unsecured Loans

Loans can be secured or unsecured, depending on whether they are backed up by collateral (assets that the lender can take possession of if the borrower doesn't make payments). For example, car loans and mortgages are secured loans. Your promise to repay the loan is secured by the car or house you're buying. If you fail to make your payments, the lender can seize the car or house to recoup the money it lent you. Unsecured loans are backed up only by your promise to repay, which is why they normally come with higher interest rates.

Revolving Credit

Revolving credit refers to loans for which the amount borrowed changes over time, unlike non-revolving credit (regular loans), where you borrow one amount and then pay it back. With revolving credit, there's a maximum you can borrow (usually referred to as *credit limit*), and a minimum payment you must make each month, but the rest is up to you. Credit cards and home equity lines of credit (HELOCs) are the most commonly used types of revolving credit.

CREDITORS AND DEBT COLLECTORS

Your Rights and Responsibilities

Your creditors only make money if you pay them, so they'll often try to work with you to help you avoid becoming delinquent on your bills. Call your creditors before you miss a payment. Waiting until your account is already delinquent will hurt your credit score and your credibility. The creditor may not be as willing to work with you and may turn your account over to a debt collector. Creditors are also quicker than ever to report late payments to collection agencies because more and more people are filing for bankruptcy and walking away from their debts. If you make arrangements with the creditors ahead of time, they may agree to not report your delinquency to the credit bureau.

Make a Plan with a Budget

When negotiating with creditors, don't agree to a plan that you're not sure you can stick to. Look at your budget and figure out how much money you can squeeze out of it each month to apply to the account in question before committing to a payment plan.

If you talk to a creditor over the phone, take good notes, including the name of the person you spoke to, the date and time you spoke, and what arrangements were made. It's a good idea to then follow up with a letter outlining the key elements of your discussion, and to ask that they send you something in writing as well. If you're not successful in getting the creditor to work with you, hang up and try calling again. Sometimes one customer service representative or credit manager will be more helpful or flexible than another.

Debt collectors are third parties hired by a lender to attempt to collect amounts you owe when you're late with your payments; they can be lawyers or companies in the business of collecting unpaid accounts. If your account gets turned over to a debt collector, you can save yourself a lot of grief if you're familiar with your rights under the Fair Debt Collection Practices Act, the federal law that specifies what third-party debt collectors can and cannot do. Collectors:

- Are allowed to contact you in person, by mail, telephone, email, or fax.
- Are not allowed to contact you at inconvenient times, such as before 8 a.m. or after 9 p.m., unless you agree to those times.
- Can't continue calling you if you've asked them in writing to stop.
- Can't threaten, harass, badger, or abuse you or use false or misleading information.

When you get a call or a letter from a debt collector, your instincts will probably tell you to either respond or ignore it. Both of those options are mistakes and can come back around to hurt you. If you communicate at all with the collector about the debt or if you pay any amount toward the debt, you have officially acknowledged the debt. If you ignore every communication, which may include court summons, you could end up with a judgment against you that allows the collector to garnish your wages.

The right way to handle collections is to start by requesting a validation letter, which must be provided within five business days of the first contact. That letter must include full details on the debt, complete contact information for the collections company, and an explanation of how you can challenge the debt.

Verify the Debt

Collectors may have incorrect information. Collectors also may lie (there are many scammers in this space). Demand proof of the debt they're trying to collect, and make sure it is both legitimately yours and correct. Once you've asked them to verify the debt, they have to leave you alone until they provide the information you requested. If they don't send you proof of the debt, you can demand that they stop contacting you with a cease and desist letter.

If it really is your debt, find your records from the original creditor (whoever you owed the money to initially) along with proof of any payments you made. You can use this information to help negotiate a settlement or payment plan if you can't pay the debt in full right away.

If the debt isn't yours or isn't 100 percent correct, dispute it. If you challenge the claim within thirty days of the collector's first contact, they must stop asking for payment until the dispute has been settled. If you file the challenge after that thirty days is up, they can keep contacting you during the investigation period.

Record or Document Everything

Any time you communicate with the debt collector, keep a full record. Keep copies of everything you send to them, and only send written communications through certified mail (so you have proof they received it). When you speak with them, either record the call (with their knowledge) or take detailed notes during the conversation. Document the date and time of the call, the collector's name, and everything you discuss.

Be careful what you say to them. They will use anything you say to help them collect. Don't talk with them about your paycheck, your budget, or other bills you have to pay. Keep the conversation focused on the specific debt they're collecting, but do not accept responsibility for the debt until you have verified that it's real and correct.

FILING FOR BANKRUPTCY

The Last Resort

Bankruptcy is a federal court process that places you under the protection of the bankruptcy court while you try to repay your debts (Chapter 13 bankruptcy) or removes the debts altogether (Chapter 7 bankruptcy). When you file for bankruptcy, an automatic stay goes into effect; the stay prohibits your creditors from attempting to collect the debt without the approval of the court, even if the bank is in the process of foreclosing on your house. Filing for Chapter 13 in this situation could buy you the time you need to sell the house yourself and pay off the mortgage.

Before you resort to bankruptcy, there may be things you can do to improve your situation. If your debt isn't totally overwhelming, you may be able to cut back on nonessentials and find the money to apply to the debt. You may even want to sell your car or house and buy a less expensive one. If you haven't taken advantage of the latest low mortgage rates, refinancing your mortgage (again) may net you a few hundred dollars a month that you could put toward your debt.

As a last resort, you could apply for a hardship withdrawal from your 401(k) plan if your plan allows them. The CARES Act expanded provisions for hardship withdrawals necessary due to COVID-19. If you've been affected by the virus, you can apply for a special hardship withdrawal of up to $100,000 without paying the normal 10 percent early withdrawal penalty. Other special COVID-related provisions include:

- No mandatory 20 percent income tax withholding.
- The option to pay the income tax on the withdrawal with your 2020 taxes or spread it evenly over the next three tax years.
- The ability to put that money back within three years.

If you're thinking about taking money out of your 401(k), contact a trusted financial advisor to help you work out the best way to do it.

CHAPTER 13 BANKRUPTCY: REORGANIZATION

Chapter 13 bankruptcy involves reorganization of your debts. You'll need to file a proposal with the bankruptcy court detailing your plan for repayment and include a detailed budget, which could be challenged by the court if the judge, the trustee, or a creditor feels you've padded it with nonessentials. You'll have to use all of your disposable income (any money left over after you pay for absolute necessities like power and water) to cover debt payments. If you want to spend money on anything else, you need permission from the court. If the court accepts your proposal, it may garnish your wages during the repayment period, which usually lasts three to five years. In Chapter 13 bankruptcy, you can prevent the loss of your home by immediately starting to make your regular mortgage payments and any catch-up payments required by your repayment plan.

Before you make the decision to file for bankruptcy, you should know which debts you may be able to walk away from and which you'll still be responsible for. Debts that can't be discharged or forgiven include:

- Child support and alimony
- Debts for personal injury or death caused by drunk driving
- Most student loans

- Traffic tickets and other fines or penalties imposed for breaking the law
- Certain types of taxes owed
- Debts you forgot to list in your bankruptcy papers

Harder to File Bankruptcy

In 2005, Congress drastically changed the bankruptcy system. The Bankruptcy Abuse Prevention and Consumer Protection Act of 2005 passed, which made it more difficult for individuals to seek shelter in bankruptcy. Among other changes, it has become harder to qualify for Chapter 7, and financial counseling sessions are required.

Eligibility for Chapter 13

Because repayment of some of your debts is the basis for this type of bankruptcy, you have to have enough regular income to cover the monthly payments. Regular income can include Social Security benefits, childcare or alimony, and rental income, and, of course, employment or self-employment wages. You also have to be up-to-date on your income tax filings. You also can't exceed the current Chapter 13 debt limitations, which change every three years. For 2020, the limitations are $1,257,850 of secured debt and $419,275 of unsecured debt.

CHAPTER 7 BANKRUPTCY: LIQUIDATION

Under Chapter 7, liquidation, you turn most of your personal property over to the court, which appoints a trustee to sell the property and use the proceeds to pay off all or some of your debts. You may be allowed to keep certain exempt property (such as your house or your car), but that depends partly on your home state, your equity in the property, and whether you're current on the payments. This entire process takes about six months to complete. At the end, all of your debts will be fully discharged except for a few types that remain on the books (more on that in a minute).

Is Chapter 7 Bankruptcy an Option for You?

After the Bankruptcy Abuse Prevention and Consumer Protection Act of 2005, Chapter 7 bankruptcy became difficult to qualify for. Now, if the court determines that you have enough disposable income, you'll be required to file a Chapter 13 bankruptcy instead. You also may not be eligible to file Chapter 7 if you've previously filed for bankruptcy within the past six to eight years.

Chapter 7 might be a good option if you have a lot of credit card or other unsecured debt, few assets, and low income. Talk with a credit counselor and an experienced bankruptcy attorney before taking this step; there may be other ways to handle your debts that will give you more control over your situation.

Debts That Can't Be Forgiven or Discharged

Some debts, such as child support and taxes owed, cannot be erased by bankruptcy. In most—but not all—cases, student loan debt will not be discharged under Chapter 7. In addition, you will almost certainly be held responsible for debts challenged by your creditors. These include:

- Debts you incurred by fraud, such as those obtained with false information on a credit application
- Credit purchases over a certain dollar amount in the sixty days prior to filing
- Loans or cash advances over a certain amount in the months prior to filing
- Debts you incurred by purposely damaging someone else's property

You will also remain responsible for any debts you don't list in your court filing, so if you go this route, make sure to include every debt you have when you fill out the paperwork.

Chapter 7 bankruptcy stays on your credit report for up to ten years from the day you file. During that period, you may be denied credit or charged higher rates for loans or credit cards. Using credit responsibly moving forward can help rebuild your credit, but that won't happen overnight. Use care when taking on new debt, and make sure you can afford to make every payment on time.

DEBT MANAGEMENT

If you filed for bankruptcy because of irresponsible money management, it won't help you in the long run if you don't change your spending habits. On the other hand, if your bankruptcy was caused by job loss, high medical bills, disability, death, divorce, or other circumstances not entirely in your control, filing may give you a fresh start. If you file for bankruptcy, the court will place restrictions on how you can spend money and will not allow you to buy what it considers nonessentials.

Chapter 13 bankruptcy can actually help you learn financial discipline that may prevent you from ending up in the same situation again, because you'll live under a strict budget for the entire repayment period, which is typically between three and five years.

The ten-year period following the filing of bankruptcy may be difficult, as the bankruptcy follows you around whenever you apply for credit or even sometimes when you apply for a job.

AVOIDING FINANCIAL SCAMS AND SCHEMES

Be aware that there are many disreputable people who call themselves credit counselors but who really just prey on desperate people. Do plenty of research to make sure you're dealing with a reputable company before you hand over any personal information or sign anything. It can sometimes be hard to tell the good guys from the bad guys in the credit counseling universe. Avoid any companies that:

- Won't send you free information
- Don't disclose their fees up front
- Ask you for money before they'll talk with you
- Promise they'll increase your credit score
- Promise they can stop pending or potential lawsuits

If you notice even one of these red flags, do not work with that company.

Credit Repair Scams

You're in debt up to your ears, the debt collectors are hounding you every time you turn around, you can't get any new credit, and along comes a credit repair clinic that promises to clean up your credit history in days. Doesn't it sound too good to be true? If someone says that you can improve your credit score overnight, it's a scam. Repairing poor credit isn't quick and easy. Anyone who promises you that it can be is lying.

Avoid working with anyone who offers up any of these as a poor credit solution:

- Starting over with a new Social Security number, which is illegal
- Giving you a new "credit identity" and a credit profile number (CPN), which is illegal
- Removing negative but true information (such as bankruptcies) from your credit report, which is illegal
- Guaranteeing a fixed increase (like 200 points) in your credit score, which is a lie

The truth is that the only way to repair poor credit and increase your credit score is by paying down your debt and developing good financial habits. Anyone who tells you otherwise is scamming you.

Payday Loans and Advance-Fee Loan Scams

When you're in an immediate financial fix, a payday loan can seem like a lifeline, but that financial "rescue" comes at a very steep cost. These loans come with extremely high interest rates—the annual percentage rates (APRs) can come close to 400 percent!—that can pull you into a dangerous cycle of needing to borrow more just to get by.

Here's how it works. In exchange for a postdated personal check or an authorization to directly pull money from your checking account, a payday lender essentially gives you an advance on your next paycheck that has to be paid back right away (usually no longer than two weeks). For this convenience, the lender charges you a fee for every $100 borrowed. The way they word it makes it seem as if you're not paying a crazy amount, just $10 or $15 per $100. But it really takes a much bigger toll on your finances.

If the lender charges you $15 for every $100 you borrow, that seems like a 15 percent interest rate. But because the loan has to be paid back in two weeks, the APR is really 390 percent (15 percent divided by 2 weeks times 52 weeks). In comparison, even the highest-rate credit cards don't have triple-digit APRs—and that's part of what makes payday loans so toxic to your finances.

Current Scams

The FTC's website at www.ftc.gov lists current scams and unscrupulous schemes. Before you get involved in anything that sounds too good to be true, check it out with the FTC or one of the consumer groups online that monitor fraud.

Since you have to pay the lender back when you get your paycheck, you won't be able to use that paycheck to cover your expenses, which forces you into taking another payday loan. If you can't pay it back, the lender can get a judgment against you and garnish your wages. Breaking the cycle can be very hard, and the only way to get out is to stop borrowing money this way. You'll need to find other ways to get your hands on cash even if it means borrowing from family.

Chapter 5

Student Loans

If you're among the 69 percent of people with student loans, there's a lot you need to know about repayment and how to keep your interest costs as low as possible. If the thought of paying off the large balances seems overwhelming, or if you're struggling to make the payments, you have options available to you to make it easier.

TYPES OF LOANS

What to Know Before You Sign Up

The most common type of student loan is a direct loan. These are either subsidized, meaning the federal government pays the interest while you're in school and during grace and deferment periods, or unsubsidized, which means you're responsible for interest from the day you take out the loan. If you didn't make any interest payments while you were in school, you'll end up with a larger loan balance to pay than the amount you borrowed, because that interest was added to the balance of your loan. A larger loan means your monthly payments will be higher, and you'll pay more interest over the life of the loan.

Grace Periods

The day after you leave school, whether you graduate, withdraw, or drop to less than half-time status, your grace period begins (usually at least six months). During your grace period, you don't have to start making monthly payments. Your first loan payment will be due at the end of your grace period, but that doesn't mean you can't start making payments sooner. If you're not sure when you have to make your first payment, check with your loan servicer.

Deferments and Forbearances

If you're having trouble making student loan payments, you have options other than default (where you just stop paying). Deferment is one option for relief during a period of financial difficulty. If you qualify for a loan deferment, you won't be required to make principal payments on your loan during that period. If you have an unsubsidized direct loan, you'll be responsible for making the interest payments yourself during the deferment period, or the interest will be added to your loan balance. If you have a subsidized loan, the federal government will make the interest payments for you. You can qualify for a deferment under the following circumstances:

- Unemployment
- Enrollment in school at least half-time
- Active military duty
- Serving in the Peace Corps
- Financial hardship
- Rehabilitation program due to disability

If you don't qualify for a deferment, you may qualify for forbearance, a special arrangement with your lender that allows you to reduce or postpone principal payments temporarily. Interest continues to accrue during this period on both subsidized and unsubsidized direct loans, and if you don't pay it during the forbearance, it will be added to the balance of your loan. This costs you more in the long run.

Don't Be Late

Late student loan payments are reported to the credit reporting bureaus just like late credit card, mortgage, or car payments. This information may stay on your credit history for up to seven years, unless you rehabilitate your loan.

Contact your loan servicer to request forbearance. You may have to fill out a general forbearance application, or they may grant it over the phone (it's at their discretion whether or not to grant it, but they usually do). There's no time limit on the forbearance, but you should try to keep it as short as you possibly can. While this is a better option than defaulting on your loan, it's still a costly choice. The longer you remain in forbearance, the bigger your debt will grow. If you can, use the reduced payment option rather than the total pause for your forbearance to prevent your financial situation from getting even worse.

To request a deferment or forbearance, you have to complete an application available from your lender. Some lenders provide these online. Within thirty days of submitting your application, you'll be notified in writing whether or not your deferment or forbearance was approved.

HOW TO MAKE YOUR PAYMENTS MORE MANAGEABLE

The sooner you start paying off your loans and the larger your monthly payment, the less your loans will cost you in the long run. If you find yourself having difficulty making your loan payments, it's better to be proactive than to make late payments or default on your loans. Call your lender at the first indication that you may have trouble making payments.

There are several options for making your loan payments simpler. One is loan consolidation: This option allows you to combine all of your eligible student loans into one loan with a single payment. Another option, if it's financially possible, is to prepay all or part of your student loans at any time without penalty, which can greatly reduce your interest costs.

Repayment Options

If you have federal student loans and you can't afford your full monthly payment, you may be able to change your payment plan. There are several options available:

- **Standard repayment:** You pay the same amount each month over ten years or less, which results in lower interest costs than most other options, except prepayment.
- **Graduated repayment:** You repay the loan over the same period (ten years), but the payments are smaller for the first two years and grow increasingly larger in later years. Because the lower payments include mostly interest and you don't pay the balance as quickly, you'll pay more interest over the life of your loan.
- **Pay As You Earn (PAYE) plan:** Monthly payments are calculated every year to equal 10 percent of your discretionary income (according to US Department of Education guidelines), but never more than they would be under the standard plan.
- **Revised Pay As You Earn (REPAYE) plan:** Monthly payments are calculated every year to equal 10 percent of your discretionary income (and can be more than standard plan payments).
- **Income-Based Repayment (IBR) plan:** Monthly payments are calculated every year to equal 10 percent of your discretionary income (15 percent if your loans are from before July 2014).
- **Income-Contingent Repayment (ICR) plan:** Payments equal the lesser of 20 percent of your discretionary income or what your monthly payments would equal calculated over twelve years.
- **Income-Sensitive Repayment (ISR) plan:** Your loan term is increased to fifteen years, and your monthly payments are recalculated annually based on your income.
- **Extended repayment:** You can use this plan if you owe more than $30,000 in federal student loans. It gives you lower monthly payments by extending your loan term for up to twenty-five years.

MANAGING STUDENT LOANS

Some Strategies

To be considered for student loans, you will need to check "yes" in the section of your Free Application for Federal Student Aid (FAFSA) form that asks about interest in student loans.

Interest rates on federal student loans range between 4 and 7 percent (those rates may change every year) for the life of the loan, generally with a ten-year loan term. No interest payments are required while you're a student, as long as you attend at least half-time, though interest may accrue on your loan during that time. There's a six-month grace period after you graduate, drop below half-time status, or leave school for any reason. Repayment begins at the end of the grace period and is made directly to the loan servicer.

Terms of the Loan

You may be able to receive a deferment or forbearance on a Perkins Loan by applying to your college. During a deferment, you can temporarily postpone payments without accruing interest. If you're not eligible for a deferment, you may qualify for a forbearance, which allows you to reduce or postpone payments for a limited period of time. Interest will accrue during this period, and you'll be responsible for paying it.

Part of your Perkins Loan may be forgiven or canceled if you work full-time in certain occupations, such as teaching full-time at a low-income school or in certain subject areas where there's a teacher shortage.

PLUS LOANS

Parents of dependent students can also take out loans called PLUS Loans. To qualify, the parent must pass a credit check and will be held liable for the loan. Graduate students can apply on their own, and approval is based on their own credit score. The interest rate is fixed (the rate as of April 2020 was 7.08 percent), and repayment must begin sixty days after the loan is disbursed. The Federal Direct Loan Program will charge a 4.248 percent origination fee, which will be added to the loan amount.

KEEP TRACK OF THE INTEREST RATES

Federal Direct Loan interest rates and fees are clearly displayed online at www.studentaid.gov. Congress periodically adjusts how interest is charged (fixed or variable) and the maximum interest rates that will be in place every school year. Make sure you're looking at the most up-to-date information as you research your loan.

Consider having federal student loan payments automatically deducted from your bank account each month to shave 0.25 percent off your interest rate and to ensure you're never late with a payment.

DEFAULTING ON YOUR STUDENT LOAN

Student loans are the first real debt many people incur. Late payments or defaults can seriously harm your credit record for many years, but if you pay on time you can build a positive credit history that will help you qualify for a home mortgage, new car loan, or other type of credit. The federal government has made it increasingly difficult to escape your student loan debt, and there is no statute of limitations, so you can be sure it will dog you forever if you don't pay.

What Constitutes a Default?

If you don't make payments for 270 days (around nine months), you'll be considered to be in default of your federal student loan (timelines may be different for private loans). Once you're in default, your loan servicer will file a default claim with the guaranty agency, which buys your account from the lender and assigns the loan to a collection agency. You'll lose all the protections and options that come with federal student loans. The government also notifies all the credit bureaus.

Consequences of Default

If you don't pay your defaulted loan right away, you could have your federal income tax refunds withheld and applied to the loan balance, have your wages garnished, have collection costs of up to 40 percent of the loan levied against you, and face possible legal action. If you have a professional license or certificate of any kind (medical, law, accounting, and so on), it could be revoked. You may no longer be eligible for federal financial aid programs. You also lose your eligibility for federal loans such as FHA and VA loans, which enable many people to buy a house that they wouldn't qualify for otherwise, and you may be denied credit cards or other forms of credit. The government may even sue you and take your car, bank accounts, and other valuable property that you own and place a lien on your house, if you own one. The default will show up on your credit report for seven years and could affect your ability to rent a house or apartment, buy a car, qualify for a mortgage, or even find a job.

Preventing Default

If you're having trouble making your loan payments, you have several options. You could change your repayment plan, apply for deferment or forbearance, or apply for a loan consolidation that could reduce your monthly payments. If you've tried everything and are still having problems with your loan, contact your borrower advocate, who can act as a liaison between you and your lender and may be able to help find solutions to your problem. Lenders really don't want you to default on your loan, and they'll usually offer you a few alternatives—you just have to ask before it's too late.

REHABILITATING YOUR DEFAULTED FEDERAL LOAN

Once you've defaulted on your student loans, any unpaid interest is computed and the entire balance of the loan becomes due and payable immediately. Once you reach this point, you have several options to avoid the negative consequences of default:

- You can pay off your entire student loan in one lump sum.
- You can establish monthly payment arrangements with your guaranty or collection agency (rehabilitation).
- You can consolidate your account into one new loan.

When you come to a repayment agreement with your lender, guaranty agency, or collection agency, a new loan is created that wipes out the old, defaulted loan. Options may be different if you have private student loans rather than federal loans.

The Process of Rehabilitation

Rehabilitation is a federal repayment program offered to student-loan holders who have defaulted on their loans. To rehabilitate your loan, you have to make nine on-time monthly payments in a row. Then your loan will be removed from default status. You can only rehabilitate a defaulted student loan once.

Regaining Your Student Loan Benefits

Besides removing your loan default from reports to the credit reporting bureaus, rehabilitating your loan helps you regain your student loan benefits if you still need them and restores your eligibility for student financial aid.

RESOLVING STUDENT LOAN DISPUTES

Sometimes errors occur in student loan record keeping. If you believe there's an error in your student loan—an incorrect balance, payments not credited, incorrect interest rate, incorrect personal information, or other error—contact the servicer that holds your loan. If you can't resolve the issue on your own, as a last resort you can contact the Federal Student Aid (FSA) Ombudsman of the Department of Education by calling 1-877-557-2575 or writing to US Department of Education, FSA Ombudsman, PO Box 1843, Monticello, KY 42633. You can also fill out an online request for assistance through the FSA Feedback System at www.studentaid.gov.

CONSOLIDATING STUDENT LOANS

The Possibility of Combining

Decisions about student loan repayments can significantly impact your finances long into the future, so before you jump into a consolidation loan, research your options and make sure you're going to achieve your purpose without any costly surprises.

BENEFITS OF CONSOLIDATING

If you have several student loans (and many people do), you may want to consolidate them after you graduate just to simplify your record keeping and bill paying. You may also want to take advantage of the longer repayment period and lower overall payment that you may get from consolidating. Consolidating may be a good option for you if you have heavy education debt, want to lock in at a fixed rate, or want to reduce your monthly payments and are willing to pay more over the length of your loan in order to do so.

Under the Federal Direct Loan Program you can consolidate your federal student loans at a fixed interest rate with only one payment a month. The interest rate on consolidation loans is a weighted average of the interest rates on all your student loans, so you'll basically be paying the same overall interest rate. The federal program also allows you to extend the term of the loan up to thirty years. Be aware that a longer loan period will cost you much more in interest, but there are no prepayment penalties, so you can always pay more or pay the loan off early.

Before you extend your loan repayment period, use an online calculator to calculate the true cost over time.

You May Not Need to Consolidate

You can consolidate all your loans with one lender at any time without a consolidation loan if you just want to simplify your payments. If a lower interest rate is your goal, remember that after making forty-eight consecutive on-time payments, you may qualify for an interest rate reduction. This may put you at a lower rate than you could get by consolidating, depending on your current interest rate. To figure out what makes the most sense for you, try Sallie Mae's online loan consolidation calculator in the tools and calculators section at www.salliemae.com.

You can also consider refinancing to get a better interest rate.

A TAX BREAK

Up to $2,500 a year in interest on most student loans may be tax-deductible, if you meet certain criteria, such as income limits. You must have used the proceeds of the loan for qualified higher education expenses (tuition, fees, room and board, supplies, and other related expenses), and you must have been enrolled at least half-time in a qualified program at an eligible institution.

As of tax year 2019, deductibility phased out if your income was between $65,000 and $80,000 for single taxpayers and $135,000 and $165,000 for couples filing jointly. These limits are increased from time to time to adjust for inflation, so see IRS Publication 970 for up-to-date limits. Unlike the mortgage interest deduction, you don't have to itemize in order to get this deduction. If you're married, you have to file jointly.

MAKING COLLEGE MORE AFFORDABLE

If you're starting a family of your own, you may want to consider ways to help your children pay for education. You may want to keep your children's student loans minimal. If so, it's never too early to look at strategies for making higher education more affordable.

Saving for College

One way to help children pay for college is to accumulate funds that can be used to pay for their education. You can do this in a variety of ways, but the best ways include college savings plans and certain types of retirement accounts.

529 Plans

Section 529 college savings plans are sponsored by each state for the purpose of helping people save for education. That education includes college, graduate school, trade school, and private K–12 schools. These plans have become popular for their tax benefits, high contribution limits, and flexibility.

You can put away a lot of money in a 529—hundreds of thousands of dollars—and the maximum contribution depends on your state laws. If you use your state's 529 plan, you may be eligible for a state income tax deduction for your contributions. Furthermore, the earnings in the account grow tax-free, so the balance can grow more quickly. Finally, if you spend the money on qualified education expenses (which are defined quite broadly), you don't have to pay any income tax when you take the money out. However, if you use the money for unqualified expenses, you will have to pay taxes and possibly penalties on the earnings portion of the withdrawal.

Qualified educational expenses include:

- Tuition
- Fees
- Supplies and equipment (such as textbooks) required for classes

Expenses that are *not* qualified include:

- Room and board
- Transportation
- Insurance
- Medical expenses

If your child does not go to college, you can always transfer the funds toward another family member without penalty. You can even use the funds yourself—for a graduate degree, for example.

Keep in mind that if nobody uses the funds for higher education, you may have to pay taxes and penalties on any account earnings that you withdraw. The penalties may be reduced or eliminated, however, in the event that your child gets a scholarship and doesn't need the money.

Coverdell Education Savings Accounts (ESAs)

You can contribute up to $2,000 per year per beneficiary (future student) in this type of account, formerly known as an "Education

IRA." This can add up, especially if you have several children (or grandchildren), since you can contribute $2,000 annually to separate ESAs set up for each child (or grandchild). Annual contributions are allowed up until the account beneficiary turns eighteen.

If you are unmarried, your ability to make ESA contributions is phased out between adjusted gross income (AGI) of $95,000 and $110,000. For joint filers, the phaseout range is between $190,000 and $220,000. ESA earnings build up tax-free, and then the money can be withdrawn (also tax-free) to pay the account beneficiary's K–12 school or college expenses. If withdrawals exceed eligible education expenses, the earnings portion of the withdrawal would be taxable. Like contributions to Roth IRAs (Individual Retirement Accounts that are not taxed upon distribution), ESA contributions are nondeductible, but the tax-free withdrawal privilege makes up for that. If the beneficiary doesn't attend college, doesn't incur enough expenses to exhaust his or her account, or is about to turn thirty, the balance can be rolled over tax-free into another family member's ESA or into a 529 plan. If the ESA hasn't been used or transferred by the time the beneficiary turns thirty, taxes and penalties may apply.

Eligible expenses include:

- Tuition and fees to attend private and religious schools
- Room
- Board
- Uniforms
- Transportation
- Books and supplies
- Academic tutoring
- Computers, peripheral equipment, and software
- Internet access charges

You have until April 15 of the following year to make your ESA contribution for the tax year in question. For example, you can make your 2020 ESA contribution as late as April 15, 2021.

Other Strategies

If you think that you or your child will have to borrow to pay for education, set the stage early. Keep an eye on how assets are titled as soon as possible. Assets in your name or the child's name can affect how your child qualifies for loans, scholarships, and gift aid. If your parents want to help their grandchild, plan ahead on how their assets can accomplish this. For example, 529 accounts can often receive favorable student aid treatment, so have Grandma and Grandpa consider 529 contributions.

If you're self-employed and your kids are old enough to do some work, put them to work. You can pay them for tasks such as filing, stuffing envelopes, and cleaning. You'll get a tax deduction, and they'll have earned income that they could put into a Roth IRA. For example, the child could fund a Roth IRA, and take the contributions (but not the earnings) back out without incurring any taxes or penalties at college time. Though income or assets in the child's name may hurt his or her chances of receiving needs-based financial aid, retirement accounts are not usually considered for this purpose.

As well, consider sending your offspring to a local community college for the first two years of his or her education. Much of those two years will be taken up with general education courses, and tuition will generally be much less than at a four-year school. The student can then transfer to a four-year college or university for the last two years of study.

Chapter 6

Working—Finding the Income You Need

Salary is not always the most important indicator of job potential. Knowing how to evaluate a prospective employer, determine your worth in the job market, negotiate the best salary and benefits, and request a raise will help you optimize job potential. In today's volatile market, it's equally important to know how to protect yourself financially if you lose your job.

WHAT KIND OF JOB DO YOU WANT?

Finding the Total Package

Salary is a very important factor in choosing a job, but it's not the only thing to consider. Evaluate the total compensation package: salary, insurance, paid leave, retirement plan, and other benefits, which can add up to tens of thousands of dollars in non-salary compensation. Once you've placed a dollar value on the employer-provided benefits, evaluate other aspects of the job. Remember that there are some things you can't put a price tag on, such as training and experience.

EVALUATING A POTENTIAL EMPLOYER

When evaluating a potential employer, find out as much as you can about the industry. What's the history of growth in the industry and what's the anticipated future need for goods and services produced or provided by that industry? Is the industry trendy? Is it subject to government regulation? If so, what's the possible impact on the company?

Don't Get Stuck

There may be times when you need a job—any job—and you don't have the luxury of being selective, but you don't have to stay in one that's a dead end. Continue your search even after you find employment if the job doesn't provide you with what you need.

Also find out as much as you can about the company or organization. In addition, if you know anybody who has worked for the organization, find out what you can about the company culture and atmosphere and the quality of management.

Evaluating the Job

What do you know about the job itself? Is there a training program or opportunity to obtain additional education? What are the day-to-day tasks and duties? Who will you report to and what is that person's leadership style? What are your potential coworkers like? Does the job require travel, weekend work, or working long hours? What is the salary and benefits package? If the salary seems low, are there benefits that compensate for it?

YOUR WORTH TO AN EMPLOYER

Before you enter the job market, whether it's your first job out of college or a new step on your career path, you need to know what the going salary is in your geographical area for someone with your education, training, and skills. You can find some salary information online at websites like *Glassdoor* and *Indeed*. For a more in-depth view, the *Occupational Outlook Handbook* produced by the Bureau of Labor Statistics (BLS) is an invaluable source of information on salaries in hundreds of different occupations. It also provides descriptions of what workers do on the job, working conditions, training and education needed, and expected job prospects in a wide range of occupations. In addition, the BLS provides information on wages, earnings, and benefits for many occupations by region, state, and metropolitan area. Visit BLS online at www.bls.gov.

YOUR SALARY AND BENEFITS

Getting What You're Worth

Much has been written about negotiating salary and benefits, but most of it boils down to knowing what you're worth in the marketplace, identifying which benefits are important to you, and putting a price tag on the benefits offered by your prospective employer so you can evaluate its real value. When meeting with prospective employers, find out what benefits and perks the company gives employees in the position you're applying for, what an average pay increase is, and what benefits the company might add if they're not able or willing to offer the salary you'd like.

Experts caution job seekers to delay discussing salary until well into the interview process and to avoid telling interviewers your current salary. You shouldn't be pegged at a salary range that's lower than the going rate just because you're underpaid in your current job, and discussing salary too early in the process can stick you with a lower than acceptable offer or, conversely, take you out of the running if your current salary is too high.

Cost of Living Calculator

To find out how much you'd need to earn in a new city to equate to your current salary, use the cost of living calculator at www.smartasset.com. Enter the city and state you're moving from and to, your current gross salary, and basic information about your family size.

EVALUATING YOUR
EMPLOYEE BENEFITS

Employer-provided benefits are a significant part of any compensation package and can have a profound effect on your finances. Employers often provide a wide range of benefits, including the following:

- Retirement plans, such as the 401(k)
- Group health, life, dental, and disability insurance plans
- Tuition reimbursement
- Flexible Spending Accounts (FSAs)
- Health Savings Accounts (HSAs)
- Stock option plans
- Bonus plans
- Vacation, holiday, and sick-leave benefits (also called paid time off or PTO)

All of these benefits, as well as others not mentioned, have a monetary value that you should consider when evaluating your salary or comparing job offers. Some benefits, such as 401(k) plans, also have tax advantages that can save you additional money by reducing your current income tax bill.

Insurance Coverage

Most people with health insurance are covered under a group plan offered by their employer or their spouse's employer. Although employers are charging employees more as prices continue to increase dramatically each year, employer-provided health insurance is still a bargain. If you aren't offered coverage through your employer, you can purchase an individual policy, but these can be expensive—unless you qualify for subsidies under the Affordable Care Act—especially as you get older or if you have a family. Whether you're married or single, you need health insurance to protect yourself against financial disaster in the event of a serious illness or accident.

If you're fortunate enough to have employer-provided coverage, calculate its monetary value by first finding out what the company pays for your medical, dental, life, and long- and short-term disability on a monthly or yearly basis. Some ways to ascertain this information might be to consult your employment contract, your pay stub, or ask your employer's human resources department. If you contribute to the cost, subtract your contribution from the total. If your contribution is pretax (as in your retirement plan), factor in your tax savings by adding your Social Security tax rate of 7.65 percent (up to $137,700 in earnings as of 2020, after which it's only 1.45 percent), your federal tax rate, and your state tax rate. Multiply the total percentage times the amount you pay toward your insurance coverage to calculate your tax savings.

For example, if you're in the 24 percent federal tax bracket and a 7 percent state tax bracket, add these two percentages plus the 7.65 percent Social Security tax. Your total tax rate is 38.65 percent. If you contribute $100 per month toward your insurance, your real cost is $61.35 ($100 × 38.65 percent = $38.65 in savings; $100 – $38.65 = $61.35).

Flexible Spending Accounts (FSAs)

FSAs, which can be either healthcare or childcare reimbursement accounts, are an employer-provided benefit that allows you to set aside pretax contributions to pay for eligible medical expenses that aren't covered by your health insurance or childcare expenses. Those medical expenses include premiums (unless they're paid with pretax money), deductibles, co-pays, and any other health cost considered an allowable medical expense by the IRS. For a complete list of allowable medical deductions, see Publication 502 on the IRS website (www.irs.gov).

You benefit from an FSA because your contributions are deducted from your gross income before taxes are calculated, thus reducing the amount of taxes withheld. If you have significant medical expenses, an FSA can help you save a lot of money, so don't overlook this great benefit. Don't contribute more than you think you'll use, because under IRS regulations, you forfeit any unused funds at the end of the year; FSAs are "use it or lose it" accounts. If you get stuck toward the end of the year with an unused balance, visit your local drugstore and stock up on bandages, blood sugar test kits, contact lenses and saline solution, and any other eligible goods you think you'll use in the coming year.

401(K) AND OTHER RETIREMENT PLANS

If your employer provides a 401(k) plan, you'd do well to participate—remember, your contributions and the account earnings are income tax–deferred. If your employer matches a percentage of your contribution, add this free money to your compensation total when calculating the value of your benefits. Many employers make matching contributions for up to 3 to 6 percent of your salary. If you earn $40,000 a year and contribute $200 a month and your employer match is 75 percent for up to 6 percent of your salary, your employer will kick in another $150 a month up to a maximum of $2,400 a year. Under this example,

your employer is actually paying you an additional $1,800 a year
($150 × 12 = $1,800).

EMPLOYEE OWNERSHIP PLANS

The world of employee stock ownership plans (ESOPs), stock option
plans, employee stock purchase plans (ESPPs), and incentive option
plans is confusing at best, and it's difficult if not impossible to evaluate
the potential worth of stock and stock options offered by your employer.
Stock options are a popular method of attracting employees into start-
up companies that are low on cash but full of future growth potential.

Stock Options

Stock option plans are a way for companies to attract, share ownership with, and reward employees. A stock option gives an employee
the right (but not the obligation) to buy company stock at a specified
price during a specified period after the option has vested. Companies
use the vesting period (usually at least five years) to motivate employees to stick around. Let's say you receive an option of 500 shares at
$10 per share and the stock price goes up to $20. You can exercise the
option and buy the 500 shares at $10 each, sell them for $20 each, and
pocket the $5,000 difference. If the stock price never rises above the
option price, you don't lose money, but you don't make any either.

Types of Plans

If you're offered stock options, be sure you understand which type they are and
how they work. You can find detailed information about the various types of plans
at the National Center for Employee Ownership website at www.nceo.org.

Employee Stock Purchase Plans

Employee stock purchase plans (ESPPs) offer employees the chance to buy stock, usually through after-tax payroll deductions during an "offering period" at a discounted price. The employee can then sell it right away and take the profit created by the discount, or hold on to it in expectation that its value will increase.

Employee Stock Ownership Plans

Employee stock ownership plans (ESOPs) are a type of benefit plan that is regulated by the federal government in which a trust is set up to acquire some or all of the stock of the company and sell the stock to employees. Because ESOPs receive tax advantages, they're not allowed to discriminate in favor of key or highly compensated employees, so most employees get to participate. The shares generally remain in the company trust until the employee leaves, then any vested shares get distributed to the employee. ESOPs are often used as a type of retirement plan, or as an exit strategy for the boss in small companies. Be cautious about investing the bulk of your retirement funds in company stock no matter how well established the company is.

Incentive Stock Options

Incentive stock options (ISOs) allow employees to purchase shares of stock at some time in the future at a specified price. The employee pays tax on the gain upon sale or disposition of the stock, not upon receipt or exercise of the option. Nonqualified stock options don't have the restrictions of other options and don't receive any special tax consideration. How these gains are taxed depends mainly on timing: the period between when the option was granted and exercised, and the amount of time the shares were held before they were sold.

PERSONAL FINANCE 101

ASKING FOR A RAISE

Finding the Right Strategy

If you have a job but aren't being paid what you're worth, you may be thinking about asking your boss for a raise. If this is the case, you need to be prepared to convince the powers that be that you not only deserve one but that you're worth it. Don't make the common mistake of basing your request on your need for more money or your inability to meet your financial obligations. Businesses do not base salary increases on employees' personal needs; they base increases on employees' worth to the company, the quality of their work, company pay scales, and budgetary concerns.

Don't Give Ultimatums

What's the number one rule for requesting a raise? Don't give ultimatums. This tactic will put your boss on the defensive, and may force you to quit your job or eat crow. Your goal is to convince your boss that you're worth more money because you do an exceptional job or you've accepted additional responsibility that warrants an increase or promotion.

EVALUATE YOURSELF

First, perform an evaluation of your skills, productivity, job tasks, and contribution to the company. Look at your job duties and performance from the company's perspective and base your approach on the company's needs. If you have a written job description, dig it out, along with copies of your last two or three written performance reviews. Jot down the major tasks you perform that may not be part of your formal job description. The goal is to show or remind your boss of your tangible contributions to the company, so make a list of your accomplishments and, if possible, the dollar value of each to the company. For example, you might say: "I saved the company $20,000 this year by researching and negotiating contracts with new vendors."

Determine the Going Rate for Your Job

Next, you need to determine the going rate, both inside and outside the company, for what you do. Ask your company's human resources department if there are company-wide salary ranges for your position and several related positions above yours. Review these, along with the salary information and compensation surveys you obtained from the BLS website. National information can give you an idea of what jobs similar to yours typically pay, but salaries vary from one region to another. Be sure to consult some local information by doing an online search for relevant salaries in your area (for example, search for "average salary marketing manager Des Moines").

Know Your Company's Policies and Financial Status

To increase your chances of getting the raise you want, you need to know several things about your company. What is the company's financial condition? Is it struggling to stay afloat? Is there a budget crisis? What is the policy on salary increases? Are all employees reviewed at the same time each year? Does your department have a budget for salaries that it needs to stay within? If so, you're in direct competition with the other employees in your department for limited funds, and you should work on making yourself stand out from the crowd.

Pick Your Time Carefully

Timing is everything. If you've only been at your job for a few months, asking for a raise probably won't go over very well. However, if you find after a few months that the company hired you at a salary well below that of others in your position and with your experience, it may pay to discuss this with your supervisor. If you've been formally or informally disciplined or chastised recently, wait at least a few months before asking for more money.

Don't ask to meet with your boss during the busiest time of the month or busiest days of the week, which for most people are Monday and Friday. It's to your advantage to arrange an appointment at a time that's convenient with your manager.

Consider Benefits in Lieu of Salary

Not all companies are in a position to raise salaries. However, your employer may be able to offer you additional benefits instead, such as extra paid leave, tuition assistance, stock options, overtime, or a promotion, if one is warranted. When comparing salaries, it's important to consider the financial value of these and other benefits and perks. If your company pays for all or part of your health insurance, this is as good as money in your pocket. The same is true of a 401(k) match.

BOOSTING YOUR INCOME

What If You Lose Your Job?

In this era of corporate takeovers, downsizing, mergers, layoffs, and, most recently, stunning corporate corruption and the COVID-19 pandemic, it's rare for someone to remain in the same job for her or his lifetime.

PREPARE FOR THE POSSIBILITY OF JOB LOSS

You don't need to be paranoid, but being prepared for the possibility of job loss will make it easier to deal with if it does happen. To be prepared, you need to know your net worth, set up a budget, save, and keep your debt low.

You should also have a feel for the stability of your job. How are your employer's competitors doing? Are they experiencing layoffs? Layoffs in your industry can be a good indication of the instability of your job, even if your employer has not yet made any cuts. If job layoffs have already occurred where you work, you should keep your resume updated and be looking around for possible job opportunities that fit your skills. Compile a list of references, with job titles, online information, telephone numbers, and addresses, and line up letters of recommendation. It's also a good idea to get contact information from coworkers, vendors, and customers to use for networking purposes.

Next, acquaint yourself with your employer's severance policy. Do laid-off employees receive severance pay? If so, is it based on years of service or other criteria? Will you be paid your accrued vacation balance upon termination? What will happen to your benefits if you lose your job? Will you be able to continue your health insurance benefits under the Consolidation Omnibus Budget Reconciliation Act (COBRA)? How much will it cost? It's foolhardy to go without at least catastrophic health insurance, so know what your other alternatives are if you can't afford to elect COBRA coverage (note that COBRA is often much more expensive than the monthly deduction from your paycheck—you have to pay the entire bill without the help of your employer). An illness or accident while you're uninsured could leave you no alternative but bankruptcy.

If the Worst Happens

If you get fired from your job, apply for unemployment on the first day so you'll receive the maximum benefits for which you're eligible. Filing for unemployment can call up negative feelings; a lot of people's feelings of self-worth are connected to their jobs, and losing a job can feel like a failure (it's not). Don't let emotions get in the way of applying for this valuable source of funds while you're looking for a new job. Your employer contributes to your state's unemployment insurance fund as well as a federal unemployment fund. You earned those benefits by working. If you need them, use them. It's just like any other kind of insurance—you file a claim when you've suffered a loss.

Unemployment benefits are typically about half of your regular earnings, up to your state's cap, paid for a maximum of twenty-six weeks. Your state's cap is based on the average wages in your state. For instance, the state maximum benefit in Massachusetts, effective October 2019, is $823 per week, while South Dakota's is $352 a week. You'll be required to prove that you're actively seeking work while receiving unemployment benefits, and you must be ready, willing, available, and able to work. Unemployment benefits are subject to federal income tax, so you'll need to claim them at the end of the year. Be prepared for the additional taxes you may owe as a result.

During a period of unemployment, resist the urge to use your credit cards unless absolutely necessary for critically important expenses. If you can't make ends meet, contact your creditors, tell them you've lost your job but are actively seeking employment, and request an arrangement that allows you to make reduced payments for a limited time.

BEING YOUR OWN BOSS

Working for Yourself

At some point in your career, you may decide that you'd like to start your own business instead of working for someone else.

DEVELOP A BUSINESS PLAN

The first thing you'll need is a business plan. This means looking at the potential need for whatever product or service you plan to offer, researching your probable expenses and income, determining the best location for your business, researching sales channels, and profiling your potential customers. There's no need to rush this process; the more developed and thorough your business plan, the better your chance of success. You can find a thorough, easy-to-navigate business plan template on the Small Business Administration (SBA) website at www.sba.gov.

Let's assume you've already thoroughly researched the viability of your idea for a business, prepared a business plan, and are confident that you have the skills, discipline, and work ethic necessary to be successful on your own. Here is what else you need to consider:

- Can you live without a steady income for an undetermined period of time? Before you give up your day job, you should have a healthy savings account to fall back on while you build a customer base, especially if the business is seasonal or cyclical.
- Will there be start-up costs? Do you have a solid, detailed estimate of what they'll be? Have you prepared a budget detailing

projected monthly costs and estimated sales? Talk to your banker and find out what financing options are available, if any, and what's required in order to qualify for them.

- Have you thought about the legal form your business will take? Read up on the subject or talk to an accountant or attorney about the pros and cons of being a sole proprietorship versus a partnership, LLC, or corporation.

- Have you familiarized yourself with the laws regulating your business and made a plan to comply with local ordinances and laws regarding business licensing, safety, workers' compensation, and sales tax?

- Have you talked to your insurance agent? If you're running a business out of your home, you may need a rider to your homeowners insurance policy. If you have employees, you'll need workers' compensation and liability insurance. If you have inventory, you'll want property insurance.

- What about the tax issues? You'll be required to file quarterly federal and state estimated taxes for yourself, or, if you have employees, you'll need to register to withhold and submit income and other taxes to the state and federal government and file quarterly and annual payroll tax returns. Who will do your payroll and prepare and file these reports? Do you need to hire an accountant or payroll service, or will you do this yourself?

Keep Up with Bookkeeping

If you're running a business, you need to keep track of the finances, and that means doing some bookkeeping. Talk to an accountant to help you get set up properly. The easiest way to manage your books is with online accounting software like QuickBooks or Xero, which can more than adequately handle everyday bookkeeping tasks (like invoicing) for most small businesses.

THE TRUE COST OF HAPPINESS

Your job is where you spend most of your waking hours. Therefore, it's a significant part of your life. Even if you just view it as a way to pay the bills, it affects you in many ways. If it makes you unhappy, evaluate the alternatives. Maybe you can afford to take a lower-paying job that you'll enjoy. If you're stressed and unhappy at work, you may be setting yourself up for bigger problems. You may have higher medical expenses down the road (for you as well as your family), which could offset the benefits of your larger paycheck. Keep the big picture in mind and consider the rest of your life as you evaluate your employment situation and choices.

Chapter 7

Housing Options

Whether you're seeking a new place to live in the same town or moving to a new city for a job opportunity or change of scenery, there are financial issues to consider before you take the plunge. The more you know about the costs associated with your move, the better you can plan for the financial impact.

WHERE DO YOU WANT TO LIVE?

The Ins and Outs of Renting

Looking for your first apartment or upgrading to a better one? Take a few minutes to think about what's important to you in your living space. Identify the things you won't compromise on. This will help you quickly rule out places that don't meet your minimum standards. If you can't find a suitable apartment in your price range, consider sharing a house or apartment with a roommate, or renting a studio or efficiency apartment.

Two to Three Months' Rent

You'll need to have two months' rent saved up before you rent an apartment: one month's worth for the security deposit, plus the first month's rent. Some landlords require that you also pay the last month's rent up front, for a total of three months' worth of rent.

How Much Rent You Can Afford

As a general rule of thumb, allow no more than 30 percent of your gross income for housing. If you're making $35,000 a year, you shouldn't pay more than $875 a month for rent. You'd be more comfortable at 25 percent, or $729 a month. If some or all of the utilities are included, you could pay higher rent.

FINDING AN APARTMENT

If you're looking in your own town, you probably know about some of the apartment complexes in your area. It's more difficult if you're moving to a new city, especially if you don't have the luxury of being able to go there to find housing before you move. A number of methods can make it easier.

Word of Mouth and Classified Ads

If you know people in the neighborhood you're considering, ask them for recommendations. You'll learn important information that might not be readily apparent when you walk through the building, such as noise levels and the safety of the neighborhood. The local newspapers in most towns and cities advertise apartments for rent. You might even grab independent newspapers that you find in coffee shops and pizza joints for a wider variety of inexpensive places. On the Internet, try www.craigslist.org or special sections of local papers' websites that have listings not found in the hard-copy editions.

Using a Real Estate Agent

The benefit of using real estate agents is that they're familiar with where the apartment complexes are and with the neighborhoods they're in. While you're searching, keep an eye out for agents who offer relocation packages with information about the city you're going to be living in. This could be helpful once you move.

Apartment-Finder Services

Apartment finders or locators are companies that specialize in knowing all the apartment complexes in a given area. They work with apartment property managers to keep up-to-date on apartment availability, and save you the time and hassle of making phone calls to each individual complex to get information. Try to avoid using an apartment-finder service that costs money. Some of them charge an entire month's rent. You can go online and easily find listings for available apartments in your area. Try sites such as Apartments.com.

THE BASICS OF RENTING

Leases, Security Deposits, Roommates

Remember four little words: Read the small print. You need to protect yourself by knowing all the rules and regulations of living in your new space and of leaving it. If there are provisions in the lease that you object to, see if you can work out a compromise with the landlord. Cross out the unwanted language for any changes the two of you agree to, initial and date the change, and have the landlord do the same. Don't rely on oral agreements. They're difficult, if not impossible, to prove.

If there's something you don't understand, ask the landlord or property manager to explain it. Don't make any assumptions. A few things you might want to ask up front are:

- Is there an on-site manager?
- What kind of routine maintenance is performed, and what am I personally responsible for?
- How much notice do I need to give when leaving?
- How is trash handled?
- What utilities and other services are included in the rent?
- Are there provisions in the lease that allow the rent to be raised during the lease term?

Don't be embarrassed if you have a lot of questions. Landlords expect questions, and once you sign the lease, it's too late. Make sure the answers you get from your landlord correspond with the lease document.

Landlord Fees

Most landlords check your credit report and usually charge you a fee of $20 to $35. Most will also verify your income to ensure that it's at least three times your monthly rent, so if rent is $800 a month, your monthly income would have to be at least $2,400.

Breaking Your Lease

Getting out of your lease before the end of the lease term can be difficult and expensive. You can be held responsible for paying the rent for the remainder of the lease. Find out if there are circumstances that would release you from your obligation. What if you got a job transfer? Had a baby? Some landlords will allow you to break the lease for a fee. Others may allow you to sublet to another tenant. Some landlords will allow you to sign a month-to-month lease. If you sign a month-to-month lease, be aware that the landlord can terminate the lease or raise the rent on short notice. Usually you're still obligated to give written notice of your intention to move out ten to sixty days in advance.

DEPOSITS AND OTHER CHARGES

When you rent a house or apartment, you're usually required to pay a security deposit equal to one month's rent, which the landlord will hold until you move out. At that time, any expenses for cleaning or repairs beyond normal wear and tear and any unpaid rent will be deducted from your deposit, and the balance will be returned to you. Most states have laws about how landlords have to treat security deposits. Usually they have to place them in an escrow account or an account separate from their normal operating account. The landlord may be required to pay you interest on the deposit, and is required to return it to you within a specified time after you vacate the apartment.

Getting Your Security Deposit Back

Get a receipt for any security or other deposits you pay. The receipt should show the date and amount paid, the name of the person you paid it to, the name of the landlord, the address and apartment number the deposit is for, and a statement that it's a security deposit. Save the canceled check for the security deposit when your bank returns it in your monthly statement. This and your receipt are the best proof that you actually paid the deposit. During the first week or so that you live in rented housing, go through every room and make a detailed list of everything that's broken, dirty, or damaged, including chips in cabinets or tubs, holes in walls, broken windows, missing or broken knobs, tears in or stains on carpets, chips or rips in linoleum, burns, and so on. If possible, take pictures of the damage. Send a copy of the list to your landlord and keep a copy with your pictures to use, if needed, when you leave.

Clean the apartment thoroughly before you move out and repair any damage you caused (beyond normal wear and tear). Remove all of your belongings and any trash. Ask your landlord to walk through the apartment with you and give you a signed statement about the condition you left it in. You may even want to take pictures of the condition of the apartment before you leave, in case you have to go to small claims court to get your security deposit back. Be sure to leave your landlord your forwarding address so he can mail your deposit.

Pet Deposits

If you find an apartment that allows pets, you may be required to pay a pet deposit in addition to your security deposit, to protect the property owner against any damages your pet may cause. Pet deposits can range from $100 to a full month's rent, and may be nonrefundable or only partially refundable depending on the state.

Some states prohibit landlords from charging extra deposits for pets or charging for credit checks. Landlords are also not allowed to charge deposits or fees for service animals or emotional support animals.

Utility Deposits and Hookup Charges

You may be required to pay a refundable deposit and nonrefundable hookup charges to one or more utility companies, including electric, gas, water, sewer, and cable TV. Many electric companies require a deposit of several hundred dollars. If you can prove you had electric service recently in your name in another location and you had a good payment record, the utility company may waive this requirement. When you move out, be sure to request your deposit back from the utility company.

RENTING WITH ROOMMATES

If you plan to rent an apartment with one or more roommates, your landlord may require separate deposits from each one of you. You have several choices. All of you can sign the lease, which will make you all jointly and individually liable for rent and damages. This means each one of you is fully responsible for all of the rent and all of the damages, if there are any. If one of you fails to pay the rent, the others will have to come up with his or her share or face eviction.

It's a good idea to design a written contract spelling out each person's responsibilities, including the amount of rent each will pay, who will share responsibility for damages, how payment for utilities will be divided, how long the rental agreement will last, and who will be liable for rent if one person leaves.

RENTERS' INSURANCE AND MOVING

The Big Picture

Most renters have the mistaken belief that they don't need renters' insurance and that the property owner is responsible for any damages to the property. The owner's coverage doesn't protect you against damage that you or your guests cause to the property. If you overrun your bathtub and water leaks into the apartment below, you're liable for the costs, unless you have renters' insurance.

The building owner's coverage also doesn't protect you against personal injury lawsuits if someone is injured in your apartment. And it doesn't provide for replacement of your belongings if they're stolen or damaged by fire or water. Renters' insurance does all of this and is well worth the cost—which is surprisingly low.

How Much Coverage Do You Need?

Even if you don't have much furniture or large household appliances, you'd be amazed at how much your belongings would cost to replace. For starters, you probably have several thousand dollars' worth of clothing. Take a detailed room-by-room inventory of your belongings, write down a brief description of each item, and estimate what it would cost to replace it. Include clothes in your inventory.

Replacement Cost or Actual Cash Value?

When buying insurance, it's a good idea to buy coverage for replacement cost rather than actual cash value. Replacement cost coverage is just what it sounds like: If something you own is stolen or damaged by fire or water, the insurance company will pay you what it will cost to replace it with an item of similar quality. Actual cost value coverage assumes that your belongings lose value with time and usage, and pays you only the depreciated value of the items.

Deductibles

The deductible is the amount you agree to pay out of pocket before the insurance company covers the rest of your loss. The higher the deductible, the less expensive the insurance. When choosing a deductible, you're deciding how much risk you're willing to take and balancing risk and cost. Most property deductibles are between $500 and $1,000 per year.

AUTOMOTIVE COSTS RELATED TO MOVING

Excise tax on automobiles is one of the biggest surprises people face when they register their car in a new city. This tax is based on the value of the vehicle and can amount to many hundreds of dollars on newer or more expensive models. When you're planning your move, check online for the cost of registering your vehicle and whether excise taxes are charged. You'll be able to see how much you can expect to pay on your particular make, model, and year. One comfort is in knowing that the tax will decrease each year as the car depreciates.

Auto insurance costs can vary dramatically from one city to the next. Obviously you'd expect rates to be higher in large cities, but the size of the city is not the only thing that determines rates. If you're thinking of moving to a new city, check online and get a quote on coverage for the make and model of your vehicle.

HOMEOWNERSHIP

What You Should Know

Buying a home is the most expensive purchase you'll ever make. It's also an emotional and potentially stressful experience for most people. There's a lot of information you have to absorb to make wise homebuying and financing decisions.

GETTING READY FOR HOMEOWNERSHIP

Before you start house hunting, you want your credit to be in great shape. Establish a record of paying your bills on time. Avoid taking out any new loans or applying for any new credit cards in the months before you start looking for a house. Pay off as much debt as possible to help you qualify for the loan and to give you more expendable income after you move in.

Check your credit report. It's the first thing a lender will do when you apply for prequalification or a mortgage. Make sure there's nothing in the report that's inaccurate or will raise a potential lender's eyebrow, and be prepared to explain any late or missed payments.

Review your entire financial situation. If you haven't already prepared a net worth statement, now's the time to do it. Ditto for a budget.

Avoid Becoming House Poor

You may think buying your dream house is worth any sacrifice, but years of doing without the enjoyment of vacations, new cars, eating out, decorating, or a myriad of other simple pleasures can make your dream house feel like a jail. It can also put a strain on your relationship with your spouse or partner. One rule of thumb is to buy a house that costs less than two and a half times your income. If your income is $50,000 a year, try to keep your home price under $125,000.

Prepare the Down Payment

A down payment is the amount of money you pay up front when you buy property, and it reduces the amount of money you need to borrow. The larger the down payment, the smaller your loan and monthly payments will be. However, it can be difficult to save enough for a sizeable down payment and closing costs that require cash (real estate transfer taxes, escrows for property taxes and insurance, title insurance, attorney fees, loan origination fees, and so on).

Use Your Equity

If you're selling a house, use any equity you have in it to apply to the down payment on the new house. You won't have access to those proceeds until the property sells, so try to time your closings in a way that doesn't leave you without a down payment and responsible for two mortgages.

One way is to go on a crash budget for a few months by cutting your spending to the bare minimum and saving as much cash as possible. Another method is to sock away all the extra money that comes your way: income tax refunds, overtime, bonuses, cash gifts, or—if you're lucky—lottery winnings.

HOW TO GET A MORTGAGE

The First Step

A mortgage is a legal contract that describes the terms of the loan obtained to buy a piece of real property. Paying your mortgage will become an important goal for you; when it's paid in full, you'll own your property outright.

PRINCIPAL AND INTEREST

Mortgage payments are divided between principal (the amount you borrowed) and interest (the cost of borrowing the money). Each month a little bit more gets applied to the principal balance. On a traditional thirty-year mortgage, the payments for the first twenty years or so will be more interest than principal. For example, on a thirty-year $100,000 mortgage at 4 percent interest, your payments the first year would total $5,729, of which $3,968 would be for interest and only $1,761 for principal. At the end of the year you would still owe a balance of $98,239. Over the life of the thirty-year mortgage, you'd repay the $100,000 you borrowed plus $71,747 in interest, for a total of $171,747.

Private Mortgage Insurance

If it weren't for private mortgage insurance (PMI), which protects the lender in case you're unable to make the payments on your loan, you might not be able to buy a house for many years. Most lenders require a 20 percent down payment, so on a $100,000 loan, you'd be required to come up with approximately $20,000 for the down payment plus another $5,000 (or more) for closing costs. PMI, which ranges between 0.05 and 2.25 percent of your loan balance annually, helps you buy a house with as little as 5 to 10 percent down and is folded into your loan payments.

Under federal law, your lender is required to automatically terminate PMI when your equity reaches 22 percent of the original appraised value of your home. To calculate what percent equity you have in your home, divide your loan balance by the appraised value and deduct this number from 100. If you bought your home after 1999, your lender must terminate your PMI when you reach 20 percent equity if you request it in writing. If you have an FHA or VA loan, PMI isn't required because the federal government has already agreed to protect the lender if you default on your loan.

TYPES OF MORTGAGES

You may think that all mortgages are alike, but they actually come in many shapes and sizes. There are several different terms, fixed-interest rate and variable-interest rate, balloon mortgages, government-backed mortgages, and more. To choose the best one for your personal situation, you should be familiar with at least these basic types.

Mortgage Terms

Most mortgages are for fifteen, twenty, or thirty years with an interest rate that's fixed over the life of the loan. Payments on fifteen- and twenty-year loans are somewhat higher than those on traditional thirty-year loans; you need a higher income to qualify for the shorter terms. The benefit of a shorter-term mortgage is that you build equity faster, pay off your mortgage years sooner, and save many tens of thousands of dollars.

Shorter or Longer?

If you can swing the payments comfortably, the shorter mortgage loan terms are definitely worthwhile. Not only will your house be paid off much more quickly; you'll save tens of thousands of dollars in interest over the life of your loan.

To illustrate the difference between a thirty-year and a fifteen-year mortgage, take the example of a mortgage for $150,000 at 6 percent. The payment on a fifteen-year loan would be $1,266 per month, and the total interest paid over the life of the loan would be $77,359. The payment on a thirty-year mortgage for the same amount at the same interest rate would be $899 per month (a decrease of $367), and the total interest paid over the life of the loan would be $173,415 (an increase of $95,916). Moreover, interest rates on shorter-term mortgages are almost always lower than those on longer-term mortgages, so the difference between the total interest paid on the two loans in the example would actually be even greater.

Adjustable-Rate Mortgages

The interest rates on adjustable-rate mortgages (ARMs) vary over time. They often start out as much as 1.5 to 2 percentage points lower than the prevailing market rates and increase (or decrease) at predetermined intervals once the introductory rate period expires. The amount of increase (or decrease) depends on the index they're tied to. The most commonly used indexes include one-year Treasury bills, LIBOR (London Interbank Offered Rate), or the CMT (Constant

Maturity Treasury). The rate is fixed for a certain period (usually between six months and five years) and then adjusted periodically, such as every six months or once a year. The amount the rate can increase at each interval is usually capped, most often at 2 percent; for example, if your rate was 3 percent, it could increase to 5 percent. In addition, most ARM loans include a lifetime rate cap, which is typically 6 percentage points. In a time of rising interest rates, it can be disturbing to know that your rate—and therefore your monthly payment—can increase every year. Before taking out an ARM, be sure that you can afford the highest payment possible under the terms of the loan. ARMs might be a good option if you know you'll only be in the house for a few years, but if you use one because you can't qualify for a conventional mortgage, you're risking the possible loss of your house.

Government-Backed Mortgages

Government loans such as FHA (Federal Housing Administration) and VA (Veterans Affairs) loans make homeownership possible for people who might not otherwise qualify for a mortgage. The federal government insures the loan, which is issued by a regular lender. FHA loans allow a smaller down payment than regular mortgages (3.5 percent rather than 10 or 20 percent), allow a higher debt percentage, and allow you to borrow the down payment and closing costs from a family member, which you can't do legally with a regular mortgage. These loans also come with mortgage insurance premiums, including an up-front fee and regular monthly payments. You'll need a credit score of at least 580 to qualify for an FHA loan. You can learn more on the FHA website at www.hud.gov.

VA loans are for active-duty military, veterans, and honorably discharged service members. Unlike other mortgage loans, these don't require any down payment (though that doesn't mean you shouldn't try to put some money down if you can). They have even less stringent requirements on the income-to-debt ratio than FHA loans. Before you can apply for a VA home loan, you'll need to get a VA loan Certificate of Eligibility, which you can do on the VA website at www.va.gov.

Even though they're insured by the government, FHA and VA loans are not always your best bet. If you have good credit, you should take a look at conventional loans from a bank or mortgage broker for comparison.

CHOOSING THE BEST MORTGAGE FOR YOU

As you can see, there are many mortgage options, so it's important to understand how each of the basic types would impact your payments. Don't underestimate the impact of interest rates on your monthly payments. A $100,000 loan at 7 percent interest for thirty years would cost $665 per month. The same loan at 8 percent interest would cost $734 per month, a difference of $24,840 over the life of a thirty-year mortgage.

For most people, a standard thirty-year mortgage is a good choice. You'll know what to expect each month, and you're not taking any wild risks. If you really want to save on interest costs, you can go for the fifteen-year mortgage.

FEDERAL TRUTH IN LENDING ACT AND THE APR

The federal Truth in Lending Act requires lenders to disclose the annual percentage rate (APR) and the total finance charges to borrowers in writing. The APR is the average annual finance charge. It's more meaningful than the interest rate alone because it includes costs such as loan origination fees, private mortgage insurance premium, and points that affect the total cost of your loan.

The APR levels the playing field by allowing you to quickly and painlessly compare loans that have different rates and fees. It's a much more accurate indicator of the cost of the loan. Be aware, however, that it can't be used as an accurate comparison of total borrowing costs on adjustable-rate mortgages.

Paying Points

Points are a percentage of the loan amount that you pay up front to "buy down" the interest rate on a mortgage. One point is 1 percent of the loan and usually lowers the interest rate by 0.25 percent. One point on a $100,000 loan would be $1,000, two points would be $2,000, and so on. A 7 percent loan with one point is not necessarily better (or worse) than an 8 percent loan with no points. Remember, you have to look at the APR to compare rates and fees. Paying points in order to get a lower interest rate may be worthwhile if you're planning to stay in the house for five years or more. The lower interest rate saves you a lot of money over the long term, but if you sell in less than five to ten years you won't have time to recoup your costs. You can see how much money buying points might save you by plugging different scenarios into an online mortgage points calculator, which you can find at www.bankrate.com and www.nerdwallet.com.

BUYING YOUR HOME

What Can You Afford?

Once you've decided you want to be a homeowner, you must determine how much house you can afford. There are two parts to this. The first is to follow a budget for at least three to six months so you know your spending habits and how much money you have to work with for your monthly payment. The second is to figure out how much you can honestly afford to borrow. Mortgage lenders want you to take out the biggest loan possible; your goal is to take out the smallest loan possible.

Calculate Your PITI

To estimate how much you can expect to borrow, use the two basic guidelines that banks and mortgage companies follow. Their main guideline is that principal, interest, taxes, and insurance (PITI) shouldn't exceed a set percent of your gross income (your pay before taxes), and they may set that as high as 30 to 40 percent. Let's say that your gross income is $50,000 a year ($4,167 per month). Your principal, interest, property taxes, and insurance shouldn't exceed $15,000 per year (with a 30 percent limit) or $1,250 per month using lender standards. However, you might want to consider how much of your *net* income (after taxes and deductions—your actual paycheck) you can afford to put toward housing. If your monthly after-tax income is $2,917 (70 percent of your gross income, for example), that mortgage payment takes up 43 percent of your net income every month.

Property taxes can vary drastically between states and even between towns in the same state. You can call the town or city tax assessor and ask what the typical taxes would be on a house that's in your approximate price range. Most states also offer online property tax estimators; find those by searching for "property tax estimator city state," with the area you're looking into. The sales listing for a home you're looking at may also yield some historical information—but that will change moving forward. Keep in mind that property taxes increase periodically, and that can increase your monthly mortgage payment, too, even if you have a fixed-rate loan.

The Debt-to-Income Ratio

Your debt-to-income ratio, or DTI ratio, measures the percentage of your gross income that goes toward paying debt. Most financial experts and lenders recommend keeping your DTI ratio under 36 percent of your gross income, but some lenders will let your DTI ratio be as high as 43 percent. You can calculate your DTI ratio by dividing your total monthly debt payments by your gross income.

What counts as debt here?

- The new mortgage payment
- Loan payments (including car, student, and personal loans)
- Credit card payments
- Alimony and child support
- Any other monthly obligations (like back tax payments)

Total up your monthly debt payments, then divide that number by your monthly gross income. For example, if your total debt payments come to $2,600 and your monthly gross income is $6,250, your DTI ratio would be 41.6 percent.

20 Percent Down Payment

Saving up for a full 20 percent down payment helps your finances in several ways. You'll get a better deal on your mortgage, you'll have a big chunk of equity from the start, and you won't be bothered with PMI, to name just a few of the financial benefits.

Check the Mortgage Calculator

Play around with an online mortgage calculator that will help you determine how much you can afford to pay for a house. *Mortgage Calculator* (www.mortgagecalculator.org) has an excellent calculator for this. You can also find home and mortgage affordability calculators on websites like *Zillow* (www.zillow.com) and *Dave Ramsey* (www.daveramsey.com).

Getting Preapproved or Prequalified

Before you start looking at houses, arm yourself with a mortgage preapproval letter from your lender. Sellers *love* preapproved buyers. That written thumbs-up from the lender shows the seller that you're serious about buying their house, that you've already figured out how much house you can afford and how much money you can realistically borrow. Plus, it benefits you as much by speeding everything up once you're ready to make an offer.

You'll need to present a heap of paperwork to the mortgage company during the application process, which may include:

- W-2 forms or other proof of income for the prior two years
- Federal tax returns for the prior two years
- Documentation for any other income you're claiming, such as overtime, bonuses, child support, or alimony

- A list of all your debts and financial obligations, such as credit cards, student loans, car loans, child support, or alimony, including the name of the creditor, balance owed, and minimum monthly payment
- Copies of bank statements
- Copies of investment account statements
- Information showing the source of your down payment

MAKING AND NEGOTIATING THE PURCHASE

Once you've found the house you want to buy, the next step is to make a bid. The bid will include the amount you are willing to pay for the house, the amount you will need to finance, and the time frame needed for the purchase. It would be wise to prequalify for the mortgage amount you feel you will need for the purchase so the seller knows you will most likely get the financing you require.

Should the seller agree to the terms of the bid, the formal contract process will begin. It is common practice at this point for the prospective buyer to arrange for a home inspection of the premises from a qualified home engineer. This way you can determine if the "guts of the place" are sound (the heating, electrical, and plumbing systems, the foundation, roofs, walls, ceilings, etc.). It would be wise to accompany the home engineer on the inspection so you can ask whether certain problems are due to normal wear and tear or are serious problems that the seller must address in the contract of sale.

The real estate contract should contain a few standard clauses, such as a list of whether certain items (window treatments, lighting fixtures, air conditioning units) are to remain on the premises after closing. In addition, the contract should contain confirmation that the heating, electrical, and plumbing systems, as well as all appliances, will be in working order for closing. All contracts should be conditioned upon two things: your ability to secure a specific amount of financing within a predetermined time period and the seller's ability to deliver a clean title.

There is also the matter of the earnest money (which can range from $1,000 to 10 percent of the home price) that must be paid to the seller's escrow company when the seller accepts the contract. Such an amount will be held in an escrow account until the closing and after the title is delivered to the homebuyer. If something goes wrong with the transaction (like the home inspection reveals severe flaws), then the earnest money should be returned to you unless it was nonrefundable (which can happen in a competitive buying market). The amount of the earnest money can be negotiated. At closing, that earnest money goes toward your down payment.

Once all parties have executed the terms of the contract, you must obtain a mortgage commitment from a financial institution (your bank) and hire a title company or attorney to perform a title search. A title search makes sure there are no claims on the property, and confirms that the seller has full ownership of the property they're selling you.

CLOSING THE DEAL

After your bank gives you a mortgage commitment and you have worked out all of the title issues present on your title report, you will be ready to schedule the closing. Just prior to the scheduled closing date, though, it is important to walk through the house to ensure that all of the seller's commitments have been fulfilled. You must bring a paid homeowners insurance policy, enough money to cover the down payment and closing costs, as well as photo identification to the closing.

The seller will prefer payment in the form of a cashier's check or a certified check. These forms of payment are guaranteed by the bank or credit union on which the check is drawn. Once you receive an executed deed, you'll get the keys to your new home!

Understanding Closing Costs

Closing costs are all of the costs associated with the transfer of the property, the processing of your mortgage, and the fees charged by those who make it all happen. Closing costs include:

- Attorney's fees (both your attorney and the lender's attorney)
- Title insurance policies for you and the lender
- Property taxes and homeowners insurance placed in the lender's escrow account (so that they're available to pay when due)
- Real estate commissions
- Lender fees such as appraisal, processing fees, points, origination fees, land surveys, and interest from the settlement date until your first payment is due
- Deed and mortgage recording fees and mortgage tax

Closing costs vary by location but are typically 2 to 5 percent of your loan, so if you're buying a $100,000 house, you can expect closing costs to be between $2,000 and $5,000. Like the down payment, closing costs must be paid at the time of purchase. Federal law requires lenders to provide you with a good faith estimate of your closing costs before you go to settlement.

ESCROW ACCOUNTS

An escrow account is a special account your lender sets up if your mortgage payments will include amounts for property taxes and homeowners insurance, and the lender or mortgage servicing company will be disbursing the money when these bills become due. If you have trouble saving for large expenses, escrow accounts can make it easier because each month you pay one-twelfth of the annual amounts needed. However, you're paying the money before it's really due and, in most cases, not earning any interest on it.

Lenders can easily make mistakes in escrow accounts, so it's important to keep an eye on them and make sure that you're not paying more than is necessary. By law, there has to be at least one month per year when the balance in your account is no more than one-sixth of your annual expenses paid from escrow. Once a year your lender will perform an escrow analysis to determine how much money should be deposited into the account for the coming year in order to cover the expenses that will be paid. If you have more than $50 in excess of what's needed, you should receive a refund. If you have a shortage, one-twelfth of the amount needed may be added to your monthly payments for the next year.

HOMEOWNERSHIP TAX SAVINGS

When you own a home, you may be able to deduct the mortgage interest and a few related costs from your taxable income by itemizing your deductions on Schedule A with Form 1040. By the end of January each year, your lender will send you a Form 1098 showing the amount of mortgage interest you paid during that year. Points you paid at closing may be deductible the first year you own your home if they meet a number of IRS requirements. If your points don't meet these requirements, you can deduct them over the life of the loan. For a complete list of the requirements and limitations on deductibility of home mortgage interest, see IRS Publication 936, *Home Mortgage Interest Deduction*.

Real Estate Property Tax Deduction

You may also be able to deduct up to $10,000 of real estate property taxes from your taxable income. If property taxes are included in your mortgage payment and paid by your lender, claim the amount the lender actually paid out during the year, not the amounts included for taxes in your monthly mortgage payments. Your lender places these funds in an escrow account for safekeeping and uses the funds to pay your real estate and insurance. Frequently real estate taxes are adjusted at the closing so that the purchaser may have actually paid more or less than the real estate taxes paid to the government in the year of closing. Your attorney's closing statement should disclose the amount of this adjustment and whether it should be added to, or deducted from, the amount paid to the government during the year in order to determine your real estate tax deduction.

If your local real estate taxes include charges for services such as trash removal or water and sewer, this portion of your taxes is not deductible. Look carefully at your copy of the real estate tax bill to determine how much you can deduct. The bill should identify services separately from taxes, which are based on the value of your property.

BE PREPARED FOR OTHER EXPENSES

Mortgage payments aren't the only expense to consider when evaluating whether you can afford to buy a house and how much you can afford to spend. There are also:

- Property taxes
- Homeowners insurance
- Repairs and maintenance
- Utilities
- Sewer and water bills
- Major appliances
- Landscaping and yard maintenance costs

Utilities can be very expensive if you live in a region of the country with extreme temperatures, such as the Northeast, where bone-chilling winters drive up heating costs, or in the South, where hot, humid summers run up air conditioning bills.

If you've been renting and are considering buying a house, try to think of all the things you'll need to buy that you didn't need when you had a landlord. You may need a lawnmower, weed whacker, chipper/shredder, leaf blower, rototiller, or other lawn and garden equipment; a washer and dryer, a new stove or refrigerator, or other household appliances; a snowblower or snowplow. Then there are the items that aren't absolutely necessary but that you'll want to have as soon as possible, such as window coverings (blinds, shades, or curtains) and new or additional furniture. If you're buying a fixer-upper, you'll need money for materials even if you intend to do most of the work yourself.

BUY LESS THAN YOU CAN AFFORD

Buy a less expensive house than you can afford. Then you'll have money for other things and won't be as likely to get in over your head with credit card and consumer debt. You'll even be able to make extra principal payments on your mortgage to pay it down faster or larger retirement account contributions to build up your future nest egg.

Most people use all the cash they can scrape together for the down payment and closing costs, and then end up having to use credit to buy the things they need or want for the new house. If you plan ahead and know how much house you can really afford, you can avoid being house poor—unable to afford anything but the house payment.

OWNING A CONDO

Some people decide to own a condo instead of a single-family home. You can share some costs with others, and you don't have to do as much of the work yourself. In exchange for these benefits, you have to pay homeowners association (HOA) dues or some similar fee. HOA dues pay for things like yard work, snow removal, and possibly even some utilities. With condo-style homes (which can be apartments or townhomes) you own your home but not the property it's on, so your HOA fees include property insurance, but not for insurance on your specific unit or anything inside it.

When shopping for a condo, make sure you consider the HOA dues in your budget. You might talk about mortgage costs with a lender, but don't forget that you'll owe an extra $100 to $500 per month for HOA dues. Higher HOA dues may mean that you get more from the HOA, but not always. Work with your real estate agent to understand how the HOA works and if it's going to be worth it.

OWNING A CO-OP

When you purchase a cooperative apartment, you do not technically own real estate (including your home). Instead you own shares in a corporation that owns the entire property. You become a tenant in a designated apartment in the building by signing a proprietary lease with the corporation. The co-op board of directors makes sure that the offering plan and the by-laws of the co-op are enforced. Each tenant is charged a maintenance fee that pays for the ongoing maintenance of the building along with real estate taxes, insurance, and the mortgage on the building. Although you do not technically own the real estate, for tax purposes you are entitled to deduct any interest associated with a co-op loan taken to purchase the premises as if it were a real estate mortgage. Additionally, any part of the monthly maintenance attributable to the payment of real estate taxes on the building or mortgage interest on the co-op's mortgage will flow to you. So you may be able to deduct those amounts as itemized deductions on your tax return. Usually, the managing agent of the co-op will issue a statement informing the shareholders as to the portion of the maintenance charge properly allocable to mortgage interest and real estate taxes. Before you purchase a co-op, it is important to analyze the financial statements of the co-op carefully in order to determine whether the current maintenance charge is sufficient to support the co-op's ongoing carrying costs.

HOME IMPROVEMENTS

Making Your House a Home

Whether you've just bought a fixer-upper and need to do some renovations, you're trying to make room for a growing family, or you just want to increase the value of your home by remodeling, you have several options for financing the improvements. Before you approach a lender, make a detailed plan of the work you want done and get bids from several contractors. Whenever you use your home as collateral, as in a mortgage or home equity loan, you risk losing it if you can't make the payments. That's why it's so important to get detailed, accurate cost estimates from reputable, experienced contractors. If the contractor's work is incomplete or shoddy and you have to hire someone else to finish or fix it, you still have to repay the loan.

Shop for financing at established financial institutions and compare rates and fees from several different lenders.

Contractors sometimes offer to arrange financing with a particular lender. Avoid this; it's almost always a bad idea. The contractor usually receives a commission from the lender for the referral, and you can end up paying for it in higher interest rates or fees you wouldn't incur at your local bank or credit union.

The Best Way to Find a Contractor

Ask friends, neighbors, and coworkers who have remodeled or made home improvements that you like. Find out whether the contractor was responsive, stuck to deadlines, and addressed concerns quickly and completely. Once you've identified several possible candidates, check them out with the local Better Business Bureau or consumer protection agency to see if they've had complaints filed against them and, more importantly, whether they resolved any problems satisfactorily. The *Angie's List* website (www.angieslist.com) is another good resource for finding reputable contractors in your area.

Get at least three detailed written estimates that spell out exactly what will be done, the type and quality of materials that will be used, and the cost, based on your written description of your project. Compare the bids carefully. Don't automatically choose the lowest bid without discussing each bid with the appropriate contractor so you can determine why they differ. If a bid is significantly lower than the others, you may want to toss it out. The contractor may be bidding inferior materials, planning to take labor-saving shortcuts that compromise the quality of the work, or doing a "bait and switch" where he increases the price once the work has already begun.

Contractor Fraud

Before hiring a contractor to build or renovate your home, educate yourself about contractor fraud so you know what to look out for. Visit www.homeadvisor.com for information on popular contractor scams and advice on finding and using reputable contractors.

Once you've chosen a contractor, ask for the name of his insurance agent and call to verify that he carries workers' compensation insurance and coverage for property damage and personal liability in case of accidents. You don't want to be held financially responsible if a worker is hurt on your property. It's also a good idea to call your state and local government and find out if contractors have to be licensed or bonded. If they do, check to make sure the contractor has complied. Make sure the contractor has also obtained all necessary work permits; if the contractor says those aren't necessary, go with someone else.

The Payment Schedule

Never pay a contractor the entire cost of the project up front. He'll probably request a down payment, the amount of which may be limited by state law. Try to keep the first payment to no more than one-third of the total job cost. Additional payments should be tied to completion of measurable milestones, so you're paying for the work that's actually been accomplished. Include these milestones in your contract to ensure that your contractor understands and agrees to them. You should be holding at least 15 percent of the contractor's money until the job is finished to your satisfaction and you have written proof that all subcontractors and suppliers have been paid.

Building a Home

It may be that you're not interested in improving your home but in building it yourself. This is a huge undertaking and will require a commitment of time and money.

HOME EQUITY LOANS AND LINES OF CREDIT

The two most common methods of financing home improvements are cashing out the equity in your home by refinancing and taking out a second mortgage or home equity line of credit (HELOC). Either way, you are borrowing money with your home as collateral, which reduces your equity stake and may put your home at risk (especially if housing prices decline). Home equity loans, a type of second mortgage, have a fixed term, usually between five and fifteen years, at a fixed-interest rate. You borrow one lump sum of money and make regular monthly payments over the life of the loan.

Debt Consolidation

Debt consolidation is the number one reason people use home equity loans. The loans are commonly used to pay off credit card and other consumer debt or to make home improvements. Always use caution when borrowing money against your home—you could lose it.

Home equity lines of credit are a type of revolving credit, like a credit card. They usually come with twenty-five-year terms split into two portions: the drawing period (where you borrow money as needed) and the repayment period, and they usually come with variable interest rates (rates that change periodically). You're allowed to borrow a certain amount over the drawing period of the loan, and you don't have to borrow it all in a lump sum. Some lenders give you special checks; others provide a type of credit card that you use to access the money. As you pay down the amount you've borrowed, you can borrow it again. For example, let's say you have a line of credit of $15,000. You borrow $6,000, leaving $9,000 of available credit. You pay back $3,000, making your available credit $12,000 ($15,000 – $6,000 + $3,000 = $12,000). The interest rate on HELOCs is usually variable, so your payments change depending on the current rate and your outstanding balance. At the end of the loan term, some HELOCs require you to pay the full unpaid balance; others amortize the balance over ten to fifteen years. If you sell your house, the balance is due at the time of sale.

Which Type of Loan Is Best for You?

Home equity loans are best suited for times when you need a lump sum amount. Lines of credit are best if you need the money at intervals, so you borrow only the amount you need, when you need it. Lines of credit can be dangerous if you have trouble controlling credit card debt because they work in much the same way as credit cards. But there's one very important difference: With a home equity line of credit, your home is at stake. If you get in over your head, you could lose your home.

Home equity loans are attractive because their rates are higher than interest rates on first mortgages but much lower than credit card interest rates. Interest on home equity loans may also be tax-deductible. Closing costs for home equity loans are similar to those for first mortgages. Expect to pay 2 to 5 percent of the loan amount.

The Limits of APR

You can't use the APR to compare home equity lines of credit and home equity loans. Interest rates on HELOCs are normally variable, plus the APR for a line of credit may not include fees and closing costs, so it could be misleadingly low if you try to compare it to the APR for a home equity loan.

Should You Get Your Loan Online?

A large percentage of mortgages are now done online. Lenders who offer the most competitive rates tend to be online. You will probably be able to track the progress of your loan online. At the very least, you can use the Internet to educate yourself quickly and painlessly about various mortgage products and current rates.

REFINANCING

When and Why

When you refinance your mortgage, you take out a new loan at a lower interest rate or for a different term and use the proceeds to pay off the original mortgage; you're basically replacing one mortgage with another one that will lower your current monthly payment and (hopefully) your total interest costs. Most lenders require you to have at least 10 to 20 percent equity in your home before you can refinance.

WHEN DOES IT PAY TO REFINANCE?

When mortgage rates start to drop, homeowners start to think about refinancing. While lowering your interest rate is a key factor in this decision, it's not the only thing to consider. Refinancing may make sense if you have a second mortgage or home equity loan with a higher rate, you want to take advantage of lower interest rates to shorten the term of your loan for around the same monthly payment, or because you want to trade in your ARM for a fixed-rate loan.

How can you tell whether refinancing makes good financial sense? The general rule of thumb says that interest rates should be at least 1 percentage point below your current rate, but sometimes making even a half-percentage change can be a good move. Since refinancing a mortgage comes with loan closing costs, you want to make sure that the rate change will save you more than the loan expenses. You can run those numbers using an online refinancing calculator, available on most mortgage lender websites and on sites such as *SmartAsset* and *NerdWallet*.

Credit Check

Be aware that you may not qualify for the low interest rates you see advertised. When you apply for refinancing, the lender will do a credit check, and if your credit score isn't excellent, you'll pay a higher rate.

Sometimes refinancing doesn't make sense. For example, if lowering your interest rate and monthly payment leads to paying more interest over the life of your loan (which can happen if you extend your loan term), refinancing doesn't make sense. It also doesn't make sense to refinance if you can't afford to pay closing costs out of pocket, and you need to roll them into your loan; then you'll end up paying fifteen or thirty years' worth of additional interest on those costs. Finally, if you're planning to sell your home within five years, refinancing will end up costing you more than it's worth.

Cash-Out Refinancing

Some people refinance for more than the value of their current mortgage if they have enough equity in their home. This is called cash-out refinancing, and it can damage your overall financial situation. Cash-out refinancing increases your debt and the amount of interest you'll pay to the lender (the opposite of why you would want to refinance), so consider that carefully before you choose this type of loan.

Let's say you paid $125,000 for your house, and your mortgage is $100,000. Your house has appreciated in value and is now worth

$175,000. You might refinance for $140,000, pay off the balance on your $100,000 mortgage, and take the difference of $40,000 or more in cash. You'd still have 20 percent equity in your home ($140,000 ÷ $175,000 = 80 percent), but without the cash-out your equity would stand at nearly 60 percent. If your home value declines, your equity percentage will drop even further, potentially leaving you "under water" (your mortgage loan will exceed the market value of your home).

Don't forget that your monthly payments could be significantly higher because of the higher loan balance, even though your interest rate was lowered by the refinance, so make sure you can afford them. In most cases, cash-out refinances won't serve your long-term financial health; in fact, these loans can damage your financial future. However, if you're planning to borrow anyway to make improvements to your home, this may be the way to go instead of taking out a second (possibly more expensive) loan to pay for the renovations. In the event that you cash out for purposes other than home improvements, the tax deductibility of the mortgage interest related to the refinancing may be limited. See IRS Publication 936 for the details.

TAX DEDUCTIBILITY OF MORTGAGE INTEREST

Many people do not realize that all mortgage interest isn't always fully tax-deductible, even on your primary residence (the home you live in). The government recognizes two different types of mortgage interest: acquisition indebtedness and home equity indebtedness.

With acquisition indebtedness, you may not deduct interest for more than $750,000 of debt (or $1 million of debt acquired before December 14, 2017) related to the acquisition of your primary home plus one second home. Acquisition indebtedness means a mortgage incurred in order to acquire, construct, or substantially improve a qualified home. If you also have home equity indebtedness, that loan amount has to be included in the $750,000 cap, and the proceeds must be used to buy, build, or substantially improve your home in order to be tax-deductible.

PREPAYING YOUR MORTGAGE

You can shave thousands or tens of thousands of dollars off the long-term costs of your mortgage by prepaying. There are several ways to do it. You can add a little extra to your regular monthly payment, make one extra payment a year, or pay half your regular payment every two weeks (if your lender allows that), which equates to paying an extra full payment each year.

What to Pay First

Please note that when mortgage rates are significantly lower than other consumer borrowing rates, it makes more sense to pay off any higher-interest debts (including credit cards and student loans) first. When you make extra payments, be sure to tell your lender to apply them to the principal. If you pay online, you may be able to check a box that says something like "additional principal payment," or there may be a similar line on your payment coupon (if you pay by check). Before making prepayments, check with your lender and read the fine print of your loan documents to make sure your lender won't penalize you for prepaying part of your mortgage in the first three to five years of the loan.

If you had a thirty-year mortgage for $100,000 at 4 percent interest and you put an extra $25 toward principal every month, you'd cut nearly three years off the length of the mortgage and almost $7,500 in interest.

Even if your loan does have a prepayment penalty, you'll probably be allowed to prepay up to 20 percent of your mortgage in any twelve-month period without incurring a penalty, so adding $25 or $50 to your monthly payment wouldn't trigger that penalty.

FACING FORECLOSURE

If you fail to make your mortgage payments for ninety days without communication with your lender, your lender may start foreclosure proceedings to take over your house and sell it to get back the money they lent you. If the house sells for less than you owe on it, they could sue you for the difference. A foreclosure would force you out of your home and significantly impact your credit record and your financial future, so try to take every step possible to avoid this outcome.

FORECLOSURE

How to Avoid It

There are things you can do to help prevent foreclosure. If you anticipate having trouble making payments, contact your lender immediately and explain your situation. Your lender may be willing to come up with a new payment plan that takes your current situation into consideration. You may be able to refinance the loan, extend the term, or spread the missed payments out over several months. Your lender may also offer temporary forbearance, meaning you can pause payments for a few months until you're able to start making payments again. If you have an FHA or VA mortgage, you may have other alternatives as well. Your lender doesn't want to foreclose, but they can't work with you unless you communicate with them.

THE SHORT SALE ALTERNATIVE

Short sales help homeowners experiencing financial distress quickly sell their homes for less than the outstanding mortgage. To get this process started, contact your lender. Generally you (the homeowner-seller) will qualify for a short sale only if you can demonstrate financial hardship and a house that is "underwater" financially, meaning the current market value of the property is less than the mortgage balance. The lender agrees that the sale proceeds will satisfy the full mortgage, even though it's less money, and forgives the balance. (If the lender doesn't agree to do that, you'll be on the hook for the remaining balance of the loan, and the lender can sue for payment.) Financial hardship can be due to death, disability, divorce,

PERSONAL FINANCE 101

unemployment, bankruptcy, or other life-altering circumstances. Many lenders prefer a short sale to a loan foreclosure because they usually recover more money with this option.

Tax Ramifications

Usually if a debt is forgiven, that amount will be included in the debtor's taxable income under most circumstances. However, the Mortgage Forgiveness Debt Relief Act of 2007 gives debtors relief from this provision if the loan qualifies as qualified principal residence indebtedness; this remains in force for any qualifying mortgage debt forgiven in a written agreement entered into through December 31, 2020. If a portion of your mortgage debt was forgiven, your lender will send you Form 1099-C, which you'll include as part of your income tax return for the year.

Chapter 8

Living Together and Marriage

You're tying the knot, and there are decisions to make about merging your finances. Later, you may find yourself planning for a baby, deciding if you can afford to be a stay-at-home parent, and trying to raise financially savvy kids. And although you probably don't want to consider the possibility, you may need to know how to protect yourself if your marriage ends in divorce.

GETTING MARRIED AND PERSONAL FINANCE

Merging Your Finances

Once you've decided to tie the knot, discussions about money shouldn't be far behind. You need to decide how to merge your money, what your common goals are, and so on. That will enable you to sail the waters of your relationship smoothly.

Talking about Money

People generally feel uncomfortable talking about money, even with their significant others. To take some of the discomfort out of the situation, you may want to start out by first discussing how your parents handled money and how you feel about its role in your life. For some people, money symbolizes love or security; for others, it symbolizes power or control. It can be spent freely or hoarded and saved. Explore your feelings about money together. After you've had a few initial discussions about money in general, initiate a discussion about your respective financial situations. Figure out whether either of you have any of the following:

- Large debts
- Student loans
- Credit card debt
- Child support or alimony obligations
- A bad credit record
- Past bankruptcy
- Investments

- An inheritance
- A trust fund

Get copies of your credit reports and go over them together. If your partner won't talk about money with you, consider counseling. How can you work toward common goals if one of you can't or won't talk about money? It's important to realize that each of you will probably have goals that the other doesn't share. Acknowledge that they're important too, and try to find a way to work toward these individual goals as well as those you have in common.

Making Money Matters Smooth

One of the most important things about money in a relationship is establishing common goals. Do you want to buy a house? Travel together? How will you save for the future? If you plan to have children (or already have them), what will you do about college funds? Once you talk these ideas out and come to agreed-upon conclusions, other money issues can become easier to deal with.

Who Will Do What?

How will you handle your banking? Will you keep separate bank accounts and split the bills between you? Will you share a joint account that all of your income goes into and all of your bills are paid from? It's very difficult to keep track of the transactions that two people make to a single bank account. Many couples find that a joint account for household expenses and individual accounts for each spouse's personal spending works very well ("His," "Hers," and "Theirs"). It allows each of you to have discretionary money for personal expenditures.

Often there's one person in a marriage who is more interested, motivated, or adept at paying the bills, balancing the checkbooks, tracking expenses and investments, and maintaining a budget. Talk about it. You may both quickly agree on the obvious choice for these tasks, or you may decide to share the responsibility. Regardless of who does what, sit down at least once a month and review your finances together.

Maintaining Credit in Your Own Name

Virtually all financial experts agree that after marriage you should maintain credit in your own name. Keep at least one credit card in your name only, and use it occasionally, but always pay off the balance each month. If you find yourself alone through death or divorce, you'll have a solid credit history on your own plus immediate credit available. It can be difficult to obtain credit on your own if you don't have a credit history that doesn't include your spouse.

DO YOU NEED A PRENUPTIAL AGREEMENT?

Prenuptial agreements are associated with the super-rich, but nearly everybody could benefit from one. These agreements designate how your assets and liabilities will be handled in the event of a divorce, but they can also be used to protect the interests of children from a previous marriage or spell out other important issues. If you plan to have children of your own, your agreement may contain arrangements for child support, education, or even religious upbringing.

Prenuptial agreements are appropriate for anyone who:

- Owns a business or professional practice
- Has received valuable gifts or inheritances
- Has a trust fund
- Owns a home
- Has a retirement plan
- Has substantial savings or investments
- Wants to protect the inheritance of children from a previous marriage

People in those financial situations would do well to draw up a prenuptial agreement. These agreements can be written after marriage (called postnuptial agreements), but they are usually much easier to work out ahead of time.

For a prenuptial agreement to be legally binding, each of you must have your own independent lawyer, and each must fully disclose all of your assets and liabilities.

PLANNING AN AFFORDABLE WEDDING

Keeping Things under Control

According to *WeddingWire*'s 2019 Newlywed Report, the average wedding in the United States costs around $38,700. How can you keep your wedding costs under control? First of all, make a realistic wedding budget. Make a list of everything you can think of that you'll need for the ceremony, rehearsal dinner, and reception and your estimate of what each item will cost. Refine your budget as you get price quotes, and identify the things that are most important to you. Small compromises can often add up to big savings. Most important: You don't want to start your journey as a couple drowning in debt, so make sure to keep wedding costs to an affordable level.

Plan for Tipping

Tipping is often an overlooked wedding expense that could bust your budget. Don't forget to plan for tipping caterers, limo drivers, parking attendants, and musicians 10 to 20 percent if you're happy with their services.

THE WEDDING BUDGET

The biggest factor influencing your costs is the number of guests that attend. If your average cost per person for food, drink, linens, cutlery, china, and other things you have to rent by the person is $50, knocking twenty people off your guest list will save you $1,000 plus tips.

Consider a brunch, buffet, or hearty hors d'oeuvres instead of a sit-down dinner. Bar costs can be higher than food costs, and the markup on alcohol provided by your caterer is significant. It's often cheaper to limit alcoholic drinks to beer and wine, or even to supply the booze yourself (though you may have to assume the liquor liability if the caterer won't serve your alcohol).

The busiest wedding season is May through October, and the most popular day for weddings is Saturday. Reception sites are usually less expensive if you book a wedding in the off-season (November through April) or on any day other than Saturday. Entertainers and photographers may also charge less during the off-season.

FILING TAXES AS A MARRIED COUPLE

Getting married changes the way you'll file your income taxes. You have two choices here: filing jointly and filing separately. Neither way works best for everyone; the results will depend on your unique tax situation. Some couples will pay more taxes after marriage; others will see significant tax savings. Most tax software will let you try both options to see which works out to a lower tax bill; tax professionals can also advise you to make sure you pay the least amount of taxes you legally can.

Couples who both earn a similar amount of money, no matter the amount, tend to pay more taxes than if they were each single. Couples tend to pay less taxes if their income levels are very different; for example, one partner might not work, or one partner might have an extremely high salary. These tax changes will show up on state income taxes as well as federal.

BENEFICIARIES, NAME CHANGES, AND WILLS

After the wedding, there are several legal issues you should take care of right away. Go through the documentation for your retirement plans, life insurance policies, bank accounts, and investment accounts. If you want your spouse to be the beneficiary, file change-of-beneficiary forms. Most retirement plans and life insurance policies require that your spouse be named as primary beneficiary unless a waiver is executed by the spouse. Also look for accounts you want to add your spouse's name to as joint owner, or find where you need to change the name of the person to notify in an emergency. If one of you owns property, decide whether you want to change the deed to include both your names. It should be noted that property acquired before the marriage would not be considered marital property in the event of a divorce. However, by changing the form of ownership to include both names, you have converted separate property to marital property.

If you change your name when you get married, apply for a new Social Security card, vehicle title, and driver's license in your new name. Notify banks, insurance companies, brokerages, and others about your name change. Be aware that if you add your name to your spouse's existing credit card, you'll be equally responsible for any balance that's already on the card.

Have a will drawn up or, if you already have one, have it updated or rewritten. If one of you has children from a previous relationship, it's especially important to spell out guardianship and custody issues.

CHILDREN

The Pitter-Patter of Little Feet

Your home is not the biggest investment you'll ever make—your kids are. You probably won't use cost as a determining factor in whether you decide to raise a family, but you can still benefit financially from some advance planning.

Insurance Issues

The most immediate financial issue when you and your partner are thinking of giving birth to a new member of your family is how much of the associated cost will be covered by your health insurance. Estimate how much you can expect to pay out of your own pocket, based on the coverage provided by your health insurance policy. If you're covered under an HMO, you'll probably have a co-pay for each doctor visit (usually $10 to $25) and a co-pay for the hospital admission for the delivery (usually a minimum of $250 to $500). Even if you make sure that your doctor and the hospital you plan to deliver in are in your HMO network, other professionals (such as an anesthesiologist) might not be, which could leave you facing some very large, unexpected medical bills.

Cost of Raising a Child

The US Department of Agriculture estimates that the average total cost of raising one child from birth to age eighteen runs to $233,610. That number doesn't even include any provision for college costs.

If you have a high-deductible plan instead of an HMO, you probably have to pay out somewhere between $1,500 and $8,000 before the insurance kicks in. After the deductible, your plan may pay 80 percent of all other *allowed* charges, and you'll pay 20 percent, up to a maximum out-of-pocket expense. These factors can vary, so make sure you fully understand your health insurance policy.

Find out how much it will cost to add your new family member to your group medical insurance policy as a dependent. If you and your spouse have separate insurance policies, figure out if it makes sense for one of you to transfer to the other's policy. Dependent coverage may be cheaper if you're all on one policy, especially if one spouse has employer-sponsored health insurance. If you or your spouse has the option of contributing to a Flexible Spending Account (FSA) or Health Savings Account (HSA, available with high-deductible health plans) at work, take advantage of that as soon as possible. Remember, money in an HSA stays with you until you use it, while FSA balances disappear every year (use it or lose it).

Income and Expense Issues

Think about how you'll manage on one income during maternity leave and possibly reduced income during the pregnancy. Are you covered by short-term disability insurance? If so, you'll receive between 50 percent and 100 percent of your regular income (depending on your specific coverage) for approximately six weeks following delivery (eight weeks if you deliver by C-section), or sooner if you're deemed medically unable to work during your pregnancy. Arrange childcare well in advance. It takes time to interview potential providers and check them out with other parents who have used them. Childcare is a huge expense, so figure the costs into your budget ahead of time and come up with ways to make cuts elsewhere if necessary. Childcare expenses are eligible for a tax credit as long as you provide the caretaker's employer ID or Social Security number to the IRS. If your employer offers a Dependent Care FSA (similar to a healthcare FSA but for childcare expenses), consider funding that to pay for at least some of your childcare costs with pretax dollars.

Start a baby fund to cover unexpected costs, and contribute to it monthly. Shop for bargains on baby clothes, equipment, and supplies, but don't skimp on items that affect safety, such as high-quality car seats. Babies don't care what they're wearing or what their blanket looks like, so avoid the temptation to buy every adorable thing you see (yes, it's hard).

CAN YOU AFFORD TO STAY HOME?

Before you jump to the conclusion that you can't afford to live on one salary so you or your spouse can stay home and raise your kids, consider the cost of working:

- Daycare, after-school care, day camps, babysitters
- Work clothes and shoes, dry cleaning, uniforms, special gear
- Additional wear and tear and more frequent maintenance on your car, plus gas and auto insurance
- Transportation costs such as bus fares, parking, and toll fees
- Coffee and vending machine snacks or sodas at work, office gift pools, lunches out
- Professional fees such as licenses or certificates, continuing education courses, dues or subscriptions

Estimate all of these costs, add them up, and deduct the total from your net pay (after taxes). This is how much the second income is contributing to your household budget.

For an example: Assume you bring home $400 a week. Childcare costs average around $200 per week, and those costs have been growing every year. That's already half of your take-home pay! Now subtract an estimate of all your other work-related expenses as previously listed. That's what you're really getting out of that second income. If you don't want to deal with all this math, check out articles and tips at www.parents.com.

You may find your paycheck won't stretch as far as you expected. If you can't make ends meet without the extra money, try going back to your budget and see where you can make cuts. You can find a lot of resources online offering tips and tricks for how to make ends meet while staying home with your kids. For effective cost-cutting strategies, visit websites like *The Penny Hoarder* and *The Balance*.

RAISING FINANCIALLY SAVVY KIDS

Most people end up in financial trouble by the time they're in their early twenties. That's largely due to a lack of personal financial education. You can start teaching your kids important financial concepts at very young ages. By making them comfortable and confident with money, you'll be helping raise financially savvy and secure adults.

One of the first—and most important—lessons involves opportunity cost, the concept that if you spend money on X, you won't have that money for Y. Other important lessons include delayed gratification (not getting what they want the second they want it), save first–buy later, and earning money (it doesn't magically appear). You can find helpful resources on websites like www.incharge.org and www.consumerfinance.gov (look for the Money As You Grow tab under Consumer Tools).

Kids should start receiving a "paycheck" by the time they're able to do simple chores (at around preschool age). This teaches them at a very young age how to start managing money. Encourage them to save part of their paycheck (piggy banks and clear coin jars are great for this) so they can buy something they want. You can keep a stash of prizes in the house that they can buy once they've earned and saved enough. As your kids get older, adapt your teaching to their age and ability to understand. For example, you can teach older kids about budgeting, borrowing and credit, and investing by using online tools and games. Excellent resources include Moneytopia and CashCrunch games.

Teach Good Consumer Habits

One of the most important things you can teach your kids is that advertising can influence their buying decisions. They can resist giving in to the advertiser's message that buying a particular product makes kids look cool or makes them feel good. Having the absolute latest in electronic gadgets, for example, isn't always necessary.

BREAKING APART

The Financial Impact of Divorce

Divorce affects millions of families, and dividing finances can play an enormous (and sometimes contentious) role in the process. Luckily, there are steps you can take to protect your finances both during and after divorce.

One of the biggest areas of confusion involves debt. As soon as you can, pay off (even if you have to do balance transfers) all joint credit cards and cancel them. Replace those with credit cards in just your name, so your spouse can't run up debt that you will be responsible for. Some couples obtain individual personal loans and pay off their portion of the joint debts so the accounts can be closed. If that's not possible, inform your creditors immediately in writing that you're going through a divorce, and that you would like your revolving credit accounts frozen.

Be sure to consider how divorce will impact your health insurance. If you have coverage under your spouse's policy and he or she works for a company with more than twenty employees, you're eligible to continue under the same plan for up to thirty-six months by electing COBRA coverage. You'll have to pay the amount the coverage costs the employer plus an administrative fee of 2 percent, which can get quite expensive. If you don't notify your spouse's employer of the divorce within sixty days, you lose your right to this benefit. Losing coverage through divorce also allows you to obtain coverage through the Affordable Care Act (ACA) as a special enrollment period.

Child Support

If your marriage is headed for divorce and you're the custodial parent, file for child support as soon as you and your spouse separate. Your spouse has no legal obligation to pay child support unless there's a court order from a divorce, marriage dissolution, establishment of paternity, or legal separation. An attorney or your local child support agency can help you get a court order. Child support judgments are issued as of the date of filing and are not retroactive.

Unfortunately, having a court order is not always enough. According to the US Census Bureau, only 44 percent of custodial parents receive their full child support payments regularly, and around $33 billion of court-ordered child support remains unpaid. There are routes you can take if your ex is behind on child support, but the best way to protect your family financially is to not depend on that money to cover your necessary monthly expenses. Find other secure sources of income that you can rely on to pay your bills. Even if your ex pays on time all the time, and your split is relatively amicable, situations can change and disrupt those support payments (think job loss, illness, remarriage).

That doesn't mean you shouldn't try to recover back child support if your ex-spouse is delinquent. The federal Office of Child Support Enforcement (www.acf.hhs.gov/css) offers detailed information, advice, and support for collecting back child support.

QDROS

Like all other assets in a divorce, retirement savings normally get divided. How the money gets split depends on a variety of factors, from the presiding state law (wherever your divorce proceedings take place) to relative income levels. Regardless of how the numbers work out, it's important to follow all the steps necessary to split the assets without triggering current income taxes and tax penalties, and losing a huge chunk of that money as a result.

A QDRO (qualified domestic relations order) is a special legal document that spells out how retirement plan assets will be split in a divorce. The court issues a QDRO and serves it to the employer of the spouse with the plan. That way, the spouse with the plan won't have to pay income taxes on the withdrawal. Plus, with a properly executed QDRO, the money taken out of the plan won't be subjected to the 10 percent early withdrawal penalty that normally hits premature distributions from retirement plans. And with a substantial retirement nest egg, that 10 percent could translate to an enormous amount (for example, on a $500,000 retirement account, the penalty alone would come to $50,000!).

Get the Wording Right

QDROs must contain specific information in order to be valid, so you can avoid that nasty 10 percent penalty. A proper QDRO will include the following:

- The plan owner's name and mailing address (the spouse with the account)
- The alternate payee's name and mailing address (the spouse getting the payout)
- The percentage or dollar amount of funds going to the alternate payee
- How the percentage or dollar amount was determined
- How and when the payments will be made
- How many payments will be made

You can find more details about QDRO language on the US Department of Labor website at www.dol.gov.

The Type of Plan Affects the Payout

Creating a QDRO for defined contribution plans like 401(k)s or IRAs (Individual Retirement Accounts) is pretty straightforward. Things get more complicated when defined benefit plans are involved. The calculations for defined benefit plan payments are complex and based on a variety of factors (length of service and life expectancy, for example), so the QDRO calculations are also pretty intricate. In fact, it usually requires an actuary or other retirement benefit specialist to figure out each spouse's fair share of the plan assets. On top of that, the payout terms in the QDRO can't be different than the plan's own payout terms.

Now or Later?

Many ex-spouses who receive payouts from retirement plans don't put that money back into retirement savings; rather, they use the money to cover current expenses. If the money is not put into a retirement account, it will be subject to current income taxes (unless the money is coming out of a Roth IRA account). For example, if one spouse receives $50,000 from the other spouse's plan and doesn't roll it into a retirement account, the plan manager will automatically take 20 percent for tax purposes (sort of like withholding taxes on a paycheck). That's to cover the potential income taxes on the $50,000, which will be determined by that spouse's overall financial situation at tax time.

But if that money goes straight into a retirement account, current income taxes won't apply until the money is eventually withdrawn. That offers two important financial benefits:

1. The money will grow into a more sizeable nest egg, thanks to tax-deferred compounding
2. Withdrawals will probably be smaller than the original lump sum, reducing the tax burden

Plus, it would be virtually impossible to re-create that retirement savings if the money is used to pay for current expenses. Eventually saving up another $50,000 (or whatever the amount) over time won't give retirement savings the same momentum: A great deal of compounding time will be lost.

The Roth IRA Factor

When splitting retirement accounts, remember that they're not all treated the same for tax purposes. How the account will be taxed in retirement can significantly change its fair value. For example, a $50,000 Roth IRA will be worth more than a $50,000 traditional IRA because the Roth IRA funds will be tax-free during retirement and the traditional IRA funds will be taxed.

SOCIAL SECURITY AND DIVORCE

If you're divorced, you may be entitled to receive Social Security retirement benefits based on your ex-spouse's earnings. Qualifying for the benefits depends on your specific situation and whether you meet all of the following conditions:

- You're at least sixty-two years old.
- You were married for at least ten years and have been divorced for at least two years (unless your ex-spouse is already collecting Social Security benefits).

- You're not married (it doesn't matter if your ex-spouse is married).
- Your ex-spouse *qualifies* for Social Security retirement benefits (even if he or she hasn't yet applied).
- The benefit you'd get based on your work history is less than the benefit you'd get based on your ex-spouse's work history.

If you meet all of those criteria, you'll receive up to half of your ex's full benefit. The benefits you get have no effect on the benefits that your ex-spouse gets. The opposite holds true too: If your ex-spouse claims Social Security based on your benefits, it won't have any effect on yours. Plus, neither of you can keep the other from collecting those ex-spouse benefits. In fact, your ex doesn't even need to know that you're claiming benefits based on his or her earnings history. If you've been married and divorced more than once, you can choose whichever Social Security benefit gives you the biggest payout (your or your ex's benefits).

To avoid getting reduced retirement benefits, wait until you reach your full retirement age (FRA). While you can start getting Social Security payments at age sixty-two, the monthly check will be smaller than if you wait until *at least* your FRA to start. Your FRA is based on your birth year, and you can find that information on the Social Security website at www.ssa.gov. For example, the FRA for anyone born in 1960 or later is sixty-seven.

Chapter 9

The Impact of Taxes

Filling out the forms properly is not even half the battle when it comes to taxes. You also want to avoid penalties and keep as much of your money as possible by taking advantage of every tax-saving strategy available to you. That requires a basic understanding of how taxes work and an awareness of significant tax-reduction opportunities.

BEGIN AT THE BEGINNING

The Basics of Federal and State Taxes

By having income taxes withheld from your paycheck each pay period, you're really prepaying an estimate of the taxes you'll owe for the year. You settle up your bill with Uncle Sam and any states you worked in when you prepare your tax return after the end of the year.

FORM W-4

The amount you have withheld is calculated based on a number of factors such as your filing status (married, head of household, or single), the number of jobs you have held, and the number of withholding allowances you claim on the Form W-4 you file with your employer. You should file a new W-4 with your employer if you:

- Got a big refund (more than $250) last year
- Owed over $100 last year when you filed your tax return
- Got married or divorced
- Had a child
- Can no longer claim a dependent that you claimed last year
- Started a side gig
- Bought a house

You can use the IRS online withholding calculator (www.irs.gov) to walk you through the W-4. And if circumstances change during the year, or you realize you're having too much or too little withheld, you can always fill out a new form and change your withholding.

Withhold or Save?

It never makes good financial sense to have more income taxes withheld than you know you're going to owe. Instead of giving the government a big interest-free loan all year, you could use that extra money to pay down debt faster, or have a fixed amount automatically deducted from your paycheck and deposited in a savings account.

Marginal and Effective Tax Rates

Your income is taxed based on seven taxable income brackets (sort of like buckets), ranging from 10 percent to 37 percent. The higher your income, the more tax brackets you'll cross, with the income that falls within each bracket being taxed at the rate for that bracket. You can find the most current tax brackets on the IRS website at www.irs.gov.

These brackets work the same for everyone. The first bucket's worth of income (the limits are based on your filing status) gets taxed at the lowest rate. Income that spills over from that bucket gets taxed at the next highest rate, up to that bracket's limit, until you hit the top bracket and all additional income gets taxed at the highest rate. The last bucket your income falls into tells you your marginal rate (the tax rate you'll pay on your next dollar of income).

Your effective tax rate (or average tax rate) is the tax rate you actually pay on your total taxable income (after deductions). To calculate your effective federal tax rate, divide your total federal income tax bill (not the amount that was taken out of your paycheck) for the year by your total income. Your effective tax rate lets you know how much taxes (by percent) you're really paying with respect to your total income.

STANDARD AND ITEMIZED DEDUCTIONS

When it comes to taking tax deductions, you have two choices. You can take the standard deduction, which is a fixed dollar amount that you deduct from your taxable income, or you can itemize deductions. For 2020 the standard deductions based on filing status are $12,400 if you're filing single, $24,800 for married filing jointly, and $18,650 for head of household.

If your actual allowable deductions total more than the standard deduction, you'll save money by itemizing. To see if you qualify, use a copy of Schedule A from Form 1040 to list the amounts of each of the deductions that apply to you, such as home mortgage interest, real estate taxes, state income taxes, and charitable donations. If the total is more than the standard deduction, itemizing is worth the extra work.

PREPARING YOUR TAX RETURN

For millions of people, filing tax returns brings up fear and anxiety. They're worried about making mistakes and getting audited. They're afraid they'll owe money and not be able to pay. The whole process seems overwhelming. But with tax apps and software, filing your income taxes (unless you have a complicated situation) can be a breeze.

Types of Federal Tax Return Forms

There are two versions of the US Individual Income Tax Return Form 1040: the standard form and a form designed for seniors, 1040-SR.

Most Americans will use Form 1040, also called the regular or standard form. You'll use it to calculate your total tax bill and find out whether you overpaid or underpaid during the year. If you overpaid, you'll get a refund; if you underpaid, you'll owe more money. You figure your tax bill by reporting all of your income and claiming any tax deductions and credits you're eligible to take.

Form 1040-SR makes tax filing simpler for seniors age sixty-five and older. These forms use bigger type for easier reading, and simplify the layout of the form. There is also a standard deduction table right on the form, so seniors can get the full deductions they're entitled to.

You can find either of these forms and their related instructions online at www.irs.gov.

Using Tax Software

Doing your own taxes is easy using tax software (either online or on your computer) or apps such as TurboTax, TaxAct Express, or H&R Block mobile tax app. This type of software handles both simple and complex returns with ease, and most returns can be completed and e-filed within a couple of hours. Most of these programs walk you through an interview process by asking you questions (which you can skip if you're familiar with the forms), do all the calculations, produce your finished tax return, and e-file it for you.

Using Paper and Pen

If you don't want to use tax software, you can still prepare your tax returns with pen and paper. However, if you file electronically, you can get your money more quickly, especially if you have your refund automatically deposited to your bank account. If you file a paper return, expect at least four weeks to get your refund, and even longer if you file later in the season.

HIRING A TAX ACCOUNTANT OR SERVICE

Approximately half of Americans use a tax preparation service of some type. While it pays to use expert help if you have a complex tax situation, you can save yourself hundreds of dollars (possibly thousands if your financial situation is complex) by preparing your own return. There are times when it's almost certainly a good idea to seek professional tax assistance—for instance, if you:

- Exercised incentive stock options
- Had complex investments
- Have a home-based business
- Own rental property
- Had a major life transition such as marriage, divorce, a baby, or started your own business

The qualifications of tax preparers vary immensely, and so do their fees. Certified public accountants (CPAs), tax attorneys, and enrolled agents (certified by the Treasury Department) are the only professionals who can represent you in an audit if that ever becomes necessary.

Finding a Reputable and Skilled Preparer

If you bring your tax information to five different preparers, you may end up with five different tax bills. To find a reputable, experienced tax pro, start by asking friends, family, coworkers, and other professionals for recommendations. If you can't come up with a recommendation this way, try contacting the local chapter of a professional association such as the American Institute of Certified Public Accountants (AICPA). Once you've identified someone you'd like to use, talk to her on the phone and ask about her qualifications, background, and fees. Find out whether she works full- or part-time doing tax consulting, how many years of experience she has, and whether she participates in continuing professional education. This last point is important because tax preparers need to keep up with yearly changes in tax laws. When you've made a decision, make an appointment well in advance of the filing deadline.

MAKING TAX-WISE FINANCIAL DECISIONS

Think about how much of your income goes toward taxes. If you're in the higher tax brackets, you may be handing nearly half of every dollar you earn to Uncle Sam, but there are things you can do to keep more of your hard-earned money.

Homeownership As a Tax Shelter

Owning a home may also help you reduce your income tax bill. Not only may you be able to deduct your mortgage interest and property taxes (up to $10,000) from your taxable income, you also get to keep up to $250,000 ($500,000 for married couples) of profit when you sell without paying any taxes on the gain, as long as you've lived in the house for at least two of the five years leading up to the sale.

Another way to reduce taxes is to be sure you take all the credits and other tax reductions you're entitled to, such as the child credit, education credits, head of household status, or earned-income tax credit.

TAKING ADVANTAGE OF TAX-SAVING STRATEGIES

Bunching deductions is a time-honored approach to cutting taxes. It requires an awareness of what your tax situation is before the end of the year. If you're close to being able to itemize, bunching your deductions may put you over the threshold. Bunching is a strategy that involves timing your payments of deductible expenses by pushing as many deductions as possible into one year. When you bunch, you fatten up your deductions for one year and slim them down the next year, or vice versa. If you're close to having enough medical expenses to meet the 10 percent of income requirement, and there's a medical procedure you're planning (anything from dental surgery to a medical checkup), having it before the end of the year could put you over the limit and reduce your taxes.

Refunds

Most people have too much tax withheld from their paychecks and get a refund at the end of the year. In 2018, the average federal tax refund was $2,781. That's roughly $230 per month that could have paid down debt or been deposited into a savings account.

KEEPING GOOD TAX RECORDS

You should keep detailed and organized records as though you expect to be audited. Then if you ever have to prove your income or deductions you won't be scrambling to find receipts and other documents. Without that backup, you could end up owing more taxes plus IRS penalties and interest.

Records to Keep

Hang on to any documents that identify your sources of income (W-2s, 1099s), help determine the value of assets (brokerage and mutual fund statements), and prove your deductions (receipts or invoices and canceled checks, property tax statements, mortgage interest statements, and proof of any business expenses if you file Schedule C). Checks alone may not prove the deductibility of an expense. The best proof is an itemized invoice accompanied by a canceled check proving that you paid it.

Keep your tax records in a separate file for each year. The IRS recommends keeping records for three years after the related tax return was filed, or two years after the date you paid a tax bill. Most financial professionals recommend keeping copies of your income tax returns, retirement account statements, home purchase or sale documents, and stock or other investment documents for six to ten years. You can also scan your documents, and the IRS will accept those if needed.

OTHER TAX ISSUES

Records and Audits

Even though profits (up to $250,000 for singles and up to $500,000 for married couples) on the sale of your primary residence are no longer taxable, you should keep all records related to the sale and purchase of your home(s), including settlement papers and documentation for improvements or additions to your home. To calculate whether you can claim exemption from taxes if you make a gain on the sale of your house, you have to be able to accurately document its cost basis. If you bought or built your home, the original basis is the price you paid, plus any closing costs. Improvements you make to your home increase your basis as long as they pass the IRS requirements of adding to the value of the house, extending its useful life, or adapting it to a new use. You must differentiate between improvements and repairs. Repairs can't be added to the basis of your home. If you hire contractors to do improvements, the entire cost can be used to increase your basis; if you do the work yourself, you can only add the cost of materials.

SURVIVING AN AUDIT

Even thinking about IRS audits frightens most people, but they're really not that scary (unless you've intentionally committed fraud—then you should be scared). Most audits are really about mistakes and mismatched documents, and can be solved quickly without you ever having to be in the same room as an auditor. Very few people actually get in-person audited, but millions will receive IRS letters pointing out errors that need to be corrected or explained. If you do get one of those letters, or even if you get called in for an audit, don't panic—get your paperwork together. Being prepared is more than half the battle.

The Importance of Documentation

Some characteristics of a tax return, such as having income over $500,000 or experiencing dramatic swings in income, may increase your chances of being audited. But as long as you reported everything accurately and have documentation to prove it, you have nothing to worry about.

The most basic thing you can do to reduce your chances of being audited is to make sure there are no errors on your return, which can be easy to make when you're typing in a lot of numbers. Most tax software lets you import tax documents, which cuts down substantially on mismatch mistakes. Make sure Social Security numbers for you and your dependents are accurate. If you can't file your return by the April 15 deadline, file for an extension before the deadline. Be sure to sign your return.

WHEN YOU CAN'T PAY YOUR TAXES

It can be upsetting to finish your tax return and realize you owe additional tax and don't have the money to pay it. Though you may be tempted to put off filing until you can pay, filing your tax return late will add to the problem. To avoid extra penalties, which will make your tax bill even bigger, file your tax return by the due date or file for an automatic extension even if you can't pay the full amount of tax due. Pay as much as you can to reduce future interest charges.

The IRS offers four options to help you pay off the rest of the taxes you owe. They're willing to work with anyone who truly can't pay their tax bills in full on time, but you have to be the one to contact them. The four main IRS payment options include:

- **Short-term extension to pay,** whereby the IRS grants you an extra 120 days to pay. They don't charge fees for this option, but they will charge interest. As long as your total bill is less than $100,000, you can file for the extension online on the IRS website (www.irs.gov, then choose Payment Plan under the Pay tab).
- **Installment plan,** which is like a regular loan, whereby you make monthly payments, including interest, on your debt. If you owe less than $50,000, you can apply for this plan with an online application, but there is a small fee ($31) that may be waived for low-income taxpayers. You get to choose your monthly payment amount and day (for example, you could choose to pay $125 on the fifth of every month), so make sure it's an amount you can realistically pay on time every time.
- **Temporary collection delay,** used when you're in a serious financial crisis and honestly can't afford to pay *anything* right now. This option presses pause on your tax debt and stops all collections activity and IRS actions, but you will be charged interest (and possibly penalties) until the debt is paid. To apply for a delay, call the IRS (it has to be done by phone) at 1-800-829-1040.
- **Offer in compromise,** which lets you settle your IRS debt for less money than you owe if they accept your offer (which is relatively rare). You can find out if you might qualify by using the IRS Offer in Compromise (OIC) Pre-Qualifier tool on their website. If you qualify, your next step will be filling out a lot of forms in the Form 656 Offer in Compromise Booklet and paying a $186

nonrefundable application fee. When you apply, you have to pay 20 percent of the offer up front (unless you meet the IRS Low Income Certification guidelines).

Be Prepared in the Future

To ensure that you don't owe a lot of taxes, review your withholding every year and make sure you're having enough taken out to cover your income. If you receive income that taxes weren't withheld from (such as from freelancing, or investments), make quarterly estimated tax payments or increase the amount of your withholding at work to compensate.

Estimated tax is the method used to pay tax on income that is not subject to withholding. This includes earnings from self-employment, interest, dividends, and rents; essentially any income you receive that doesn't have taxes taken out of it. The IRS website (www.irs.gov) has an estimated tax worksheet that can help figure out how much you'll need to pay each quarter to avoid getting hit with tax penalties. Estimated taxes can be paid by mail (along with IRS Form 1040-ES) or online.

You can avoid incurring tax penalties for underpaying taxes by estimating your tax liability before the end of the year to allow time to catch up if you've under-withheld. If your tax status has changed during the year, visit the withholding calculator on the IRS website to see if you need to make an adjustment. To avoid penalties, you must pay at least 90 percent of your tax for the current year before December 31, or 100 percent of your total tax liability for the prior year (110 percent if you earn more than $150,000).

If it looks as if you may not have had enough tax withheld, change your withholding by filing a new W-4 with your employer to have additional tax taken out each pay period through the end of the year. After the start of the new year, complete another W-4 to adjust your withholding back to a more normal amount.

CREDITS AND DEDUCTIONS

What's the Difference?

When managing your taxes, it's important to understand the difference between a credit and a deduction. Credits are dollar-for-dollar reductions of your income tax liability. In other words, a credit reduces the amount of tax you owe by the amount of the credit (a $500 credit reduces your tax bill by $500). Credits are usually much better for your finances than deductions.

Deductions reduce the amount of income that you get taxed on. A $500 deduction does not reduce your tax bill by $500. Instead, it reduces your taxable income by $500. You pay less in taxes, but you don't give a dollar-for-dollar reduction. If you pay taxes at 22 percent, a $500 deduction might save you $110 in taxes (22 percent of $500).

Education Benefits

Current tax law offers many education-based tax credits and deductions. These credits may be limited by your income level and other eligibility rules, but if you do qualify, they can take a huge chunk out of your tax bill.

The best way to make sure you take advantage of these benefits properly is to talk with an accountant or tax preparer. They can help you choose which combination of deductions and credits will result in the biggest tax savings for you.

American Opportunity Tax Credit

If you are in your first four years of postsecondary education, look into the American Opportunity Tax Credit (AOTC). This program offers a partially refundable tax credit of up to $2,500 per eligible student. It is one of the most powerful education benefits, as you get a dollar-for-dollar credit on the first $2,000 of qualified expenses. You'll have to qualify with certain income, enrollment, and other characteristics. For example, you have to be pursuing a degree during your first four years of higher education, and you must be enrolled at least half-time. The credit is refundable up to $1,000 in excess of your income tax liability, so those college students paying their own tuition should file an income tax return even if they had no income for the year.

Student Loan Interest Deduction

The federal government allows you to deduct up to $2,500 in the interest you paid on qualified student loans from your taxable income. It is one of several tax breaks available to students and their parents to help pay for higher education. For more information about this, visit the IRS website.

Lifetime Learning Credit

The Lifetime Learning Credit offers a tax credit even if you are in graduate school, and for some continuing education expenses related to your job. The maximum credit is $2,000, but you only get credited 20 percent against your education expenses (so you have to spend $10,000 to get the entire credit). Unlike the AOTC, this is not a refundable credit, meaning if it brings your tax bill below zero, you won't get extra money back.

Other Education Benefits

Find out if your employer will help you pay for school. Employer-provided educational assistance can be extremely powerful. If you have a family business, it can pay for somebody's schooling. Then the business can take up to a $5,250 deduction, which the recipient receives tax-free.

Interest on EE US Savings Bonds *may* be tax-free if the proceeds are used to pay for qualified education expenses. Each of these tax benefits is subject to phaseout if your income is too high. See IRS Publication 970 for details.

Tax Breaks Related to Having Children

There are many tax subsidies related to having children. Here is a short list of some of the more common tax benefits:

1. Child Tax Credit—There is a $2,000 credit available for each qualifying dependent child under the age of seventeen. This credit is subject to a phaseout if the taxpayer has too much income. See IRS Publication 972.

2. Child and Dependent Care Tax Credit—A tax credit is available for 20 to 35 percent of up to $3,000 of your childcare expenses ($6,000 if you have more than one child) each year if your child is under the age of thirteen. This could include payments made to summer day camps and after-school programs as long as you give the IRS the identification number and address of the person or entity you are paying. See IRS Publication 503 for details.

3. Earned Income Tax Credit (EITC)—Taxpayers with low earnings, especially those with qualifying children, may be eligible for this refundable tax credit, which means it makes sense to file a tax return even if you don't need to file otherwise. See IRS Publication 596 to determine if you qualify.

Chapter 10

Planning Your Retirement

You're never too young to start investing for retirement; in fact, the sooner you start, the better off you'll be. Compounding of earnings is so powerful that if you start investing in your twenties, you can amass a large nest egg with little effort by the time you are in your sixties or seventies. Getting started is easier—and less painful—than you think, especially if you have access to an employer-sponsored retirement plan. Even if you don't, it takes just minutes to set up your own retirement account and begin working toward a secure and comfortable financial future.

RETIREMENT PLANS

The Basics

Although traditional pension plans, which were in vogue half a century ago, have mostly disappeared, there are still a number of retirement plans that can help you build a big enough nest egg to live out your golden years in financial security.

DEFINED-CONTRIBUTION PLANS

Employer-sponsored defined-contribution plans don't guarantee a specific dollar amount at retirement. How much you receive depends on how much you and (possibly) your employer contributed and how well your investments performed over the years. It can't be emphasized enough that if your employer matches your contribution to a retirement plan, you should definitely be part of it. That's free money! Your contributions plus any vested contributions made by your employer are always kept in an individual account in your name.

With defined-contribution plans, you'll usually be able to choose from a variety of stocks, bonds, mutual funds, annuities, money market funds, or (sometimes) your employer's company stock. The plan will spell out how frequently you can change your investment choices. Many plans allow you to manage your account online and make investment changes as often as you like.

One of the attractive features of defined-contribution plans is that they're portable. If you change jobs, you can take your money with you. The following are the most common defined-contribution plans:

- 401(k) plans, offered by private companies
- 403(b) plans, offered by nonprofit, tax-exempt employers, such as schools and colleges, hospitals, museums, and foundations
- 457 plans, offered by federal, state, and local government agencies and nonprofit organizations

Other defined-contribution plans include employee stock ownership plans (ESOPs), profit-sharing plans, Simplified Employee Pension (SEP) plans, and Savings Incentive Match Plans for Employees (SIMPLEs). These plans all have one important thing in common: You pay no taxes on your contributions or your earnings until you withdraw the money, which you'll be required to do once you turn seventy-two.

401(K) PLANS

A 401(k) plan is an employer-sponsored retirement plan that gives a special tax break to employees saving for retirement. Here's how the tax break works: If you contribute $2,000 a year and you're in the 24 percent federal tax bracket, you'll save $480 in current income taxes for the year. Your contributions get deducted from your pay before your taxes are calculated, so you're investing with pretax dollars. If you live in one of the states where 401(k) contributions are tax deferred, and you're in a 6 percent state income tax bracket, you would save another $120 in state taxes, for a total savings of $600. The bottom line is that you add $2,000 to your investment account, but only $1,400 comes out of your pocket ($2,000 – $600 = $1,400). You don't pay taxes on your earnings until you withdraw them, presumably at retirement, so your investments grow faster as your untaxed earnings benefit from compounding.

Employer Match

Many employers match a certain percentage of your contributions. The amounts vary, but a typical match is between fifty cents and $1 for every dollar you contribute, up to 6 percent of your salary. If your employer offers matching contributions and you don't participate in the plan, it's like walking past money lying on the sidewalk and not picking it up. Even if you can't take advantage of the full match, contribute as much as you can so you'll get at least some of that free money.

Contribution Limits

The IRS sets limits, adjusted annually for inflation, on how much you can contribute to a 401(k) plan each year. For 2020, you can contribute up to $19,500. Once you reach age fifty, you're allowed to make additional "catch-up" contributions of up to $6,500.

401(k) Vesting

You always own 100 percent of your own contributions to the plan. The employer match may be subject to vesting, which means you earn the right to it gradually, over a number of years of employment with the company. About half of all employers offer immediate vesting for those matching contributions.

There are two types of vesting schedules for employers who use that method. Some 401(k) plans have cliff vesting, where you don't own any of the matching contributions until you've worked for the company for a certain amount of time, but not more than three years. The other type of vesting schedule is graded vesting, where you own an increasing percentage of the employer match over several years. By law, full vesting must take place within six years. A typical vesting schedule will now be 20 percent after the second year, 40 percent after the third year, 60 percent after the fourth year, 80 percent after the fifth year, and 100 percent after the sixth year.

It's important to consider the impact on your 401(k) when you're thinking of changing jobs. If your plan has cliff vesting, and you leave before working the required number of years, you walk away from everything your employer has contributed as matching funds. You could possibly walk away with thousands of additional dollars in company matching funds by staying in your current job for a few more months or years. Let's assume you had matching contributions of $6,000 and a vesting schedule of 20 percent per year for five years. If you left for a new job after three years, you'd take $3,600 ($6,000 × 60 percent = $3,600) of matching funds with you, plus all the contributions you made from your salary and any associated earnings, but you'd forfeit $2,400 ($6,000 × 40 percent = $2,400) plus any earnings that money has accumulated.

Switching Jobs

The portability of 401(k) plans is a great feature, but what do you do with your money when you change jobs? You have three choices:

1. If you have over $5,000 in your account, you have the option of leaving your funds in your old employer's plan.
2. You may be able to transfer your balance directly (called a roll-over) into your new employer's plan.
3. You can set up an individual IRA at a bank, through a broker, or directly with a mutual fund and roll over your 401(k) balance into that account.

The rules for rollovers are strict, so make sure you follow them carefully to avoid any tax penalties. Some plans will make a direct rollover into your new account; others will send you a check that you will need to deposit into your IRA account within sixty days to avoid tax penalties.

The Three Big Risks of Borrowing from Your 401(k)

Taking out a 401(k) loan may not seem risky, but it is. Not only can the loan derail your retirement savings; it may also take a toll on your current finances. Here are the three big risks of 401(k) loans:

1. Even though you'll pay yourself back with interest, you'll still lose all of the compound earnings on the amount you pulled out; plus, that interest rate will almost certainly be lower than the returns your money could have earned.
2. Many employers don't allow you to make contributions to your 401(k) while you have an outstanding loan, so you'll lose the ability to save; plus, repayment starts immediately and comes right out of your paycheck, which many borrowers are not prepared for. (However, under the CARES Act of 2020, you may be able to delay payments for up to one year for loans taken between March 27 through December 31, 2020.)
3. If you leave or lose your job for any reason, you have to pay the full loan back or the IRS will treat it like an early withdrawal and charge taxes and penalties.

If you're considering borrowing money from your retirement account, try to find any other way to get the money you need.

403(B) AND 457 PLANS

Defined-contribution plans, or 403(b) plans, work very much like 401(k) plans, and over time they have started to look more and more like 401(k) plans. Your contributions are tax-deductible and your earnings are tax deferred until you take the money out at retirement. Like 401(k) plans, the amounts that you and your employer can contribute are limited by law. With a 403(b) plan, employees can also take advantage of an extra catch-up contribution available if they have more than fifteen years of service. That extra contribution, known as the maximum allowable contribution (MAC), lets long-term employees contribute up to $3,000 extra per year for a total MAC of $15,000. The MAC is over and above any age-related catch-up contributions.

Section 457 plans are defined-contribution plans established by government agencies and some nonprofits. Like 401(k) and 403(b) plans, they allow you to make tax-deductible contributions, and your earnings grow tax deferred until retirement. Because 457 plans are "nonqualified" plans, specific issues such as catch-up contributions and early withdrawals are handled differently. For example, if you pull money out before age fifty-nine and a half, you won't get hit with a 10 percent tax penalty (though you will still have to pay regular income taxes on the withdrawal). Catch-up contributions work differently too. Employers have the *option* of allowing you to make regular catch-up contributions when you reach age fifty. There's also a special extra catch-up provision that employers can offer called the "last three-year catch-up." With that, you can contribute twice the regular contribution limit during the last three years before the plan's retirement age. If your employer offers both types of plans, you can contribute to both.

INDIVIDUAL RETIREMENT ACCOUNTS

A Valuable Savings Tool

Individual Retirement Accounts (IRAs) have evolved since they were established more than twenty years ago. They now include such variations as SEP IRAs, Roth IRAs, SIMPLE IRAs, and more. IRAs provide the same tax-deferred benefits as 401(k) and similar employer-sponsored plans (though Roth IRAs work a little differently) and allow you to decide how your funds will be invested.

If you have employment income (including self-employment) in any year, you can make contributions to an IRA. The annual contribution limit was $6,000 as of 2020, and you're allowed to make an additional catch-up contribution of $1,000 once you reach age fifty. You can set up an IRA through most banks and financial institutions, or through a mutual fund company or broker. You can start making withdrawals at age fifty-nine and a half, and, unless it is a Roth IRA (an IRA that isn't taxed upon distribution), you must start doing so by age seventy-two. As with 401(k) plans, income tax and a 10 percent penalty apply to any funds you take out early unless you qualify for a waiver of the penalty (for very high un-reimbursed medical expenses, qualified higher education expenses, or up to $10,000 for first-time homebuyers).

If you have access to an employer-sponsored retirement plan with matching contributions, get your match before putting money into an IRA. If you don't have access to an employer-sponsored plan, contribute as much as you can to your IRA.

Traditional IRAs

Traditional (or regular) IRAs give you a current tax deduction for your contributions, and allow your money to grow tax-deferred until you start making withdrawals. Depending on your income, your filing status, and whether you have a qualified retirement plan at work, your IRA contributions may not be fully tax-deductible. However, you can still make nondeductible IRA contributions and benefit from the tax-deferred growth inside the account even if you don't qualify for the current tax deduction. If you (and your spouse) aren't eligible for any employer-provided retirement plan, you can deduct the full contribution to an IRA regardless of your income level.

If you own a traditional IRA, you'll have to begin taking required minimum distributions (RMDs) from it starting no later than April 1 of the year following the year in which you reach age seventy-two. If you don't take your RMD every year, you could face an IRS penalty of 50 percent of the amount you were supposed to withdraw.

Roth IRAs

There are several important distinctions between traditional IRAs and Roth IRAs. Traditional IRA contributions are tax-deductible as long as you qualify with the eligibility restrictions. Roth IRA contributions are not. Traditional IRAs grow tax deferred until you withdraw the funds at retirement, and then they're taxed at your regular income tax rate. Roth IRA growth and earnings are *never* taxed, as long as you follow all the rules. Unlike traditional IRAs, there's no requirement to ever withdraw money from your Roth IRA, even after you've reached age seventy-two.

You can contribute to a Roth IRA even if you participate in an employer-provided retirement plan, and the income limits for that are higher than for deductible IRA contributions. However, high earners may be locked out of Roth contributions altogether, regardless of whether they have access to employer plans. Income limits change regularly. Visit the IRS website at www.irs.gov for the latest rules.

Choosing the Best IRA for You

It can be difficult to determine whether you'd come out ahead in the long run with a traditional or a Roth IRA. It depends on a number of factors, such as how long before you retire, when you plan to start taking money out, and your tax bracket now and expected tax rates during retirement. There are benefits to Roth IRAs in addition to tax-free earnings. You can withdraw your contributions—but not any earnings—before age fifty-nine and a half without owing taxes or penalties. You can withdraw up to $10,000 in earnings without penalty to buy your first home if the money has been in the Roth IRA for at least five tax years, to pay medical expenses exceeding 7.5 percent of your gross income, to pay college expenses for certain family members, to pay for health insurance if unemployed for at least twelve months, or if you're unable to work because of disability. Any other earnings withdrawals before the age of fifty-nine and a half will be subject to the penalty and taxes.

Regular IRA or Roth IRA?

If your income exceeds the limits for a traditional IRA (and you are an eligible participant in a qualified plan), you can still contribute, but it won't be tax-deductible. If you don't qualify for the tax deduction, then a Roth IRA is a good choice as long as your income falls under the maximum for that year. If the Roth IRA is not an option because your adjusted gross income (AGI) is too high, you can make a nondeductible contribution to a traditional IRA. When you start withdrawing from this IRA, a portion of each distribution will be considered a nontaxable return of your nondeductible contribution.

Diversify Tax Strategies

Just as you diversify your investments, you should diversify your tax strategies. Since you never know what's going to happen with tax laws in the future, you should avoid having all your eggs in one "tax basket."

As you decide how much to save in each type of account, consider your income, your prospects for the future, and your thoughts on future legislation. If you are relatively young and just starting your career, chances are that you are not earning much money (and you're therefore paying taxes at a relatively low rate). In that case, getting a deduction may not be worth much to you—and you might prefer the potential to take your money out tax-free in retirement. In addition, the ability to take back your contributions at any time may serve as a safety valve. You don't need to worry about taxes and penalties if you need to get that money back.

As you move up the income scale, a deductible contribution to your IRA or 401(k) can save you a bundle. Some people prefer to get something of value today instead of hoping for something of value later. They'd rather take a deduction because they are certain they can get it. They are not as certain about future tax law changes.

ROTH 401(K)S

Some employer-sponsored retirement plans allow Roth-type contributions. In other words, the benefits of a Roth IRA became available in some 401(k)s and 403(b)s. Previously, you could only make pretax (or deductible) contributions to these plans. For many young people, the Roth 401(k) is an attractive option.

How is a Roth 401(k) different from a Roth IRA? For starters, you can make a larger contribution into a Roth 401(k) account. You can allocate the maximum 401(k) contribution ($19,500 in 2020) toward Roth-type dollars without the AGI limitations of Roth IRAs. However, you can also split contributions—putting 5 percent of your pay in pretax and 5 percent of your pay in after tax, for example. In addition, you can contribute to a Roth 401(k) regardless of how high your income is. Unlike Roth IRAs, though, money in Roth 401(k) accounts is subject to required minimum distribution (RMD) rules, meaning you must start taking withdrawals at age seventy-two.

Roth 401(k) simply adds an additional "bucket" of money to your retirement plan. Your investment mix doesn't change—it's just the tax treatment that changes. If you leave your job, your money is still portable. However, you have to keep Roth-type money separate from traditional (deductible) money. For example, you'd roll your Roth 401(k) money into a Roth IRA, and you'd roll your traditional 401(k) money into a traditional IRA.

RETIREMENT PLANS FOR SMALL BUSINESS OWNERS AND THE SELF-EMPLOYED

For small businesses, costs are always an issue. Small employers don't have the resources that large enterprises do. However, they have to compete against larger organizations for good employees. As a result, many small businesses will offer plans that help people save for retirement while keeping costs low. SIMPLE IRAs and SEPs allow employers to offer incentives with very low administrative cost.

SIMPLE IRAs and SEPs

The Savings Incentive Match Plan for Employees (SIMPLE) IRA is a plan that may be offered by businesses with no other retirement plans and with fewer than 100 employees. As in 401(k) plans, your contributions and earnings are tax deferred. You can contribute up to $13,500 a year with an additional "catch-up" amount of $3,000 for those fifty or over. The employer must either match 100 percent of your contributions, up to 3 percent of your salary, or contribute 2 percent of compensation for each eligible employee, even those who don't contribute to the plan.

A Simplified Employee Pension (SEP) IRA is similar to a SIMPLE IRA, except that generally only your employer can contribute (some employees may be able to make traditional SEP IRA contributions). The disadvantage of this plan for most employees is the lack of control over how much money goes into your plan. However, if you're self-employed, these plans can help you save a lot of money without a lot of paperwork. In that situation, you count as both the employer and the employee at the same time. The limit on employer contributions to a SEP is 25 percent of your compensation up to a maximum of $57,000 in 2020. With both the SIMPLE IRAs and the SEP IRAs, you may also be able to invest in a personal traditional or Roth IRA. You can find full details and specific rules for setting up and funding these plans on the IRS website at www.irs.gov.

Solo 401(k) Plans

Solo 401(k) plans are among the most powerful options available to small businesses, but they only work for a one-person (or married couple) business. They share many of the characteristics of a standard 401(k) plan, including the ability to take loans. However, they are less expensive to administer. If you do any freelance or contract work, consider opening a Solo 401(k) plan. In addition to your "salary deferral" contributions, you can give yourself a profit-sharing contribution of up to 25 percent of compensation.

OTHER RETIREMENT PLANS

Finding the Right One

Nonqualified plans and other retirement benefit plans may be available to you if your skills are in high demand or if your employer is creative. For example, DB(k) plans provide a small pension-like guaranteed income stream, along with the ability to save money as you do in a 401(k). Other plans might promise you a lump sum payout every ten years or so.

CHOOSING THE RIGHT INVESTMENTS

With most retirement plans, you're in the driver's seat when it comes to choosing investments. The question is what investments to choose.

Stocks, Bonds, and Funds

Because retirement earnings grow tax deferred and you have many years before you'll make withdrawals, retirement plans are best suited for your most aggressive investing, which means putting a larger portion of this money in the stock market. You can balance some of that risk by directing part of your portfolio into bond investments. Most employer-sponsored funds offer a range of stock or bond mutual funds. With IRAs, you'll have access to a much broader choice of investments, including ETFs (exchange-traded funds), REITs (real estate investment trusts), and individual stocks and bonds.

Target-Date Funds

Many employer-sponsored retirement plans offer prepackaged options so you don't have to select individual investments and build your own portfolio. Instead, you use a model portfolio designed by an investment company. While this option may be easier to deal with, that simplicity comes at a cost, normally in the form of very high fund fees.

ESOPs

ESOPs (employee stock ownership plans) give you an opportunity to own stock in the company that employs you. These plans can be a great benefit, but there's one very important caveat: Don't put all your eggs in one basket. If company stock is the only option available to you in your 401(k) plan, look at other investment vehicles for some of your retirement savings. If you invest heavily in company stock, consider a worst-case scenario. If something bad happens to the company, it's likely that the stock price will fall. In addition, your job could be in jeopardy—if there are layoffs or if the working environment becomes unbearable. In this case you suffer a double whammy: Your retirement savings take a hit at the same time as your income.

In addition to providing diversification, many of these funds adjust their holdings over time; a target date determines how much risk the portfolio should have. For example, you might have the "XYZ 2060 Fund" as an investment option in your retirement plan. This fund might be used by a person planning to retire in 2060. When the fund has plenty of time left until maturity, it will hold a higher percentage of stocks and other riskier investments. As the years pass, the fund's managers will gradually reduce risk by adding less risky investments.

Annuities

When set up and used properly, annuities supply guaranteed steady income for life. The right annuity gives you a reliable monthly income stream that you know you can count on forever, no matter what happens in the economy or the stock market. That's especially valuable for people who can rely only on Social Security for *guaranteed* income. Annuities are insurance products. You buy (or invest in) an annuity, and the annuity pays you regularly in the future, either with monthly, quarterly, or annual payments, or in a lump sum at a specified future date.

The amount of each payment depends on several factors, including the size of the annuity, how the payments are scheduled, and for how long the payments will be made. You'll also have the option to receive payments for a certain number of years or for the rest of your life.

Like other types of retirement accounts, the money inside an annuity grows tax deferred, and you don't pay any taxes on the earnings until you start taking the payouts.

Belt and Suspenders

Annuities are useful in some situations, but they are prone to abuse. Consumers and even professionals have trouble understanding them. All annuities have a cost, and you have to pay extra for any riders (add-on features). In many cases, you have to leave your money with the insurance company for years before you can do anything else with it. Therefore, be very careful when buying an annuity.

Be especially careful about putting retirement savings into an annuity. Don't roll a 401(k) or IRA into an annuity unless you have a very good reason. Before retirement age, the most likely benefit you can get from an annuity is tax deferral. Retirement accounts already benefit from tax deferral, so annuities must offer you an additional benefit if you're going to pay the costs associated with them. Putting retirement savings into an annuity for the purpose of tax deferral is like wearing a belt and suspenders at the same time to keep your pants up.

A WORD ON SOCIAL SECURITY

Social Security is a benefit plan that's been around since 1935 for employed persons who pay into the system for the required amount of time; in other words, forty payroll quarters. In addition to retirement benefits, Social Security includes several other programs, including Medicare (the healthcare plan for people sixty-five and over), disability benefits, and survivor benefits for spouses or dependents. These programs are funded by mandatory taxes deducted from your pay and matching taxes paid by your employer.

WORKING WITH A FINANCIAL PLANNER

Consult a Professional

You may want to see a financial planner to help you chart a course for the future, or you may want to consult with a planner at a big turning point in your life. If you use a financial planner to help you choose investments, be aware that using expert advice is not a guarantee that your investments will make money. If you have the time and interest to do your own research and educate yourself, you probably don't need a financial planner for choosing investments, unless you have a complex situation. Consider developing your own written financial plans, but meet every few years with a financial planner to make sure there are no glaring issues or gaps in the course you've charted for yourself.

If you use a professional, educate yourself about the recommended investments and be involved in the buying and selling decisions she executes on your behalf. Some financial planners earn commissions on specific investments, so they may not be entirely objective when making recommendations. You can avoid this problem by choosing a fiduciary planner, who is required by law to act only in your best interests. Fee-only planners get paid by the hour or based on a fixed percentage of assets held, and they don't benefit from recommending one investment over another.

To locate a fee-only financial planner near you, visit the "Find an Advisor" page provided by the National Association of Personal Financial Advisors (NAPFA) at www.napfa.org. The site also provides valuable information about hiring a financial planner, including interview questions, an overview of the industry, and how to compare planners.

SOCIAL SECURITY AND HEALTHCARE

Benefits for Retirement

When you reach retirement age, you'll receive benefits based on a complex calculation using the number of years you worked, the income you earned during those years, and your age when you applied for the benefits. You can request a Social Security Benefits Statement by setting up a "*my* Social Security" account at www.ssa .gov. There, you'll find records of your earnings history by year (any earnings that you paid Social Security taxes on, which includes self-employment taxes), along with an estimate of the benefits you can expect to receive depending on whether you take early retirement age (from sixty-two to your full retirement age), full retirement age (sixty-seven for those born in 1960 or later), or delayed retirement age (seventy).

COUNTING ON SOCIAL SECURITY

Millions of retirees rely on Social Security as their largest source of retirement income. Collecting Social Security retirement benefits sounds simple, but it's more complicated than just signing up. To get the most out of Social Security, you'll need to do some careful planning and make some strategic decisions. Knowing how your benefits are calculated and what you can do to maximize them will help you make the best decisions for your situation.

The Social Security Administration (SSA) makes it very easy to apply for benefits online through their website www.ssa.gov. The application is easy to deal with, and it typically takes less than thirty minutes to fill out. Before you apply for benefits, you'll need to have a "*my* Social Security" account set up.

Once you're ready to apply, go to the SSA website at www.ssa.gov and click on "Retirement." Then, all it takes is three easy steps to apply for Social Security benefits.

1. Click on the "Apply for Retirement Benefits" button, then sign in to your "*my* Social Security" account. The site will take you through several screens with questions about you and your work.
2. Fill out the application. You can do the whole thing in one session or stop at any point and finish later.
3. Click on "Submit Now" to send the application electronically.

Once you're done, you'll get a receipt that you can print or save for your records. You'll be able to check the application status when it's one month until you'll start collecting benefits.

What You Pay In

If you earn income—meaning if you work for yourself or for an employer—you are paying into Social Security. All workers pay 6.2 percent of their salaries or wages (up to a set annual limit) toward Social Security every year. Employers pay an additional 6.2 percent of each worker's earnings. Self-employed people pay both parts, sending 12.4 percent of their earnings to Social Security.

HEALTHCARE

If you have health insurance, you're most likely covered under a group plan provided by your employer or your spouse's employer, or you are covered through the Affordable Care Act (ACA). No matter how old you are, you need health insurance to protect yourself against financial disaster if you become seriously ill or have an accident. If you don't have access to employer-sponsored health insurance and can't afford the premiums, you may qualify for ACA subsidies.

Good Credit Means Lower Premiums

When insurance companies price your policies, they take a lot of factors into account, and that includes your credit history. A high score and strong credit history make you eligible for lower premiums, partly because insurance company research shows that people with better credit tend to file fewer claims.

When it comes to health insurance, find a policy that covers what you need—even if it's not the cheapest policy. You won't end up saving money if your policy doesn't match the way you use medical care. For example, healthy people with no children do fine with low-cost, high-deductible policies, but families with young children may fare better with a higher-cost policy that will save them money on co-pays and wellness visits. You can find health insurance in a few different ways:

- Through the ACA exchanges at www.healthcare.gov during Open Enrollment periods or when you've experienced certain life events (such as getting married, having a baby, or losing health coverage).

- By contacting any insurance company (such as Cigna or Blue Cross Blue Shield) directly to learn about available plans in your state.
- Through a trained, licensed insurance professional who can help you find the best policy (you can find qualified professionals near you at www.healthcare.gov).

Health Maintenance Organizations (HMOs)

An HMO is an association of healthcare professionals and medical facilities that sell a fixed package of healthcare services for a fixed price. Each patient has a primary care physician, who is often referred to as a gatekeeper because services provided by a specialist are not covered unless the gatekeeper determines that the specialist is necessary.

The advantages of HMOs are lower and more predictable out-of-pocket costs and no claim forms. The major disadvantage is that services provided by healthcare professionals outside the network of your HMO aren't covered. If your network is small, your choices of doctors and other health professionals will be very limited, and services provided by specialists will be dependent on a referral from your primary physician.

Preferred Provider Organizations (PPOs)

PPOs combine the managed-care aspects of an HMO with the flexibility of a fee-for-service plan. When you use doctors in your approved network, more of your medical costs are covered, but you can go outside the network of healthcare professionals and facilities to any healthcare provider of your choice when you feel it's necessary. The main advantage of a PPO is the flexibility and a wide choice of doctors and facilities. The only disadvantages are that it's more difficult to predict your out-of-pocket costs, and you'll pay more for your healthcare if you go out of network.

Health Savings Accounts

Virtually everyone will need to pay for medical care at some point, and those costs can be outrageously high. Funding an HSA as part of your overall financial planning means that you can use tax-free earnings to pay for your healthcare expenses, saving you at least a little money. The catch is that these accounts are only available to people with high-deductible health plans.

HSAs offer a trio of solid tax benefits that boost your finances now and later:

1. Contributions reduce your tax bill now.
2. Earnings are tax-free.
3. Withdrawals are tax-free (as long as you follow the rules).

No other type of tax-advantaged account offers all three of these benefits in one. If your employer offers an HSA plan, take advantage of it. When you make contributions this way, you're funding the account with *pretax* dollars. That means your contribution does not count toward taxable income, and you don't pay tax on it; your withholding taxes are reduced.

You get the same benefit if you DIY your HSA by opening and funding an account on your own. Contributions are tax-deductible, reducing your current taxable income and your tax bill.

As long as you use the money in your HSA to pay for qualified medical expenses, your withdrawals will be 100 percent tax-free. But if you use the money for anything else, you could face tax penalties of up to 20 percent plus regular income taxes on the withdrawal amount.

And there's a beneficial twist. Once you turn sixty-five, you can use this money for anything without facing any taxes or penalties.

Be aware: HSAs come with a lot of rules. If you don't follow them to the letter, you could get hit with fines, penalties, and a bigger tax bill. Luckily (unlike many IRS rules), the guidelines for HSAs are straightforward and easy to understand. Since the rules are subject to change, check in with the IRS website (www.irs.gov) for the most current guidelines.

DISABILITY INSURANCE

Short- and long-term disability insurance protect your income-producing ability when you're unable to work due to illness or injury. Many employers provide group short-term disability insurance as a benefit at little (or no) cost to employees, with your portion paid with pretax dollars and much less than you'd pay for an individual policy. When you have both long- and short-term coverages through your employer, the policies often dovetail so that your long-term coverage would pick up as soon as your short-term coverage expires (if your disability lasts that long).

The Purpose of Disability Insurance

Although the likelihood of becoming disabled is greater than the likelihood of dying during any given period of time, more people buy life insurance than disability insurance. Before purchasing an individual disability policy, be sure you understand the terms used and read the policy carefully to make sure you know what benefits you're getting. Find out what, if any, exclusions there are, what the elimination period is, what the benefit period is, and what the definition of total disability is.

Elimination and Benefit Periods

With both types of disability insurance, there's an elimination period, which is the period of time after you become unable to work before you can begin receiving benefits under the policy. A short-term disability policy may have an elimination period of one to two weeks for illness or a shorter time for accidents. Long-term disability elimination periods are typically at least thirty days and more commonly ninety days.

If you become disabled, you'll receive benefits until you recover or reach the maximum benefit provided by your policy. Short-term disability policies pay benefits for a shorter period of time, from six weeks to two years. Long-term disability policies may pay benefits for several years or until the age of sixty-five (or longer). The shorter the elimination period and the longer the benefit period, the higher the premium will be. Most policies replace between 60 and 80 percent of your income, up to the maximum monthly benefit according to your policy.

Definition of Disability

The best policies will have a definition of disability that includes the inability to perform the major duties of your own occupation. Under these policies, if you're unable to perform your major duties, you can go to work in a different occupation that you are able to perform and still collect your disability pay. Less expensive or lower-quality policies won't pay benefits unless you're unable to do any work you're reasonably suited to do, or they'll offset your monthly benefit check against any income you're earning elsewhere. There are three types of long-term disability policies:

1. **Noncancelable and guaranteed renewable:** The insurance company guarantees that you'll be able to renew the policy for as long as you wish at the same premium and for the same monthly benefits, regardless of any changes in your occupation or income.
2. **Guaranteed renewable:** The insurance company can't drop you, but it can raise prices.
3. **Conditionally renewable:** The company can decide not to renew your policy, perhaps when you most need it, or it can raise prices and add conditions at any time.

Obviously, noncancelable and guaranteed renewable is the best type, but it will also be the most expensive. Avoid conditionally renewable policies. You want to have the assurance that your coverage will be there when you need it. Buy residual disability benefits. This means if you aren't totally disabled but can't work full-time, you'll be paid partial benefits. Expect to pay between 1 and 3 percent of your annual income for a long-term disability policy, so if you're earning $30,000, a policy will probably cost you between $300 and $900 a year. Your cost will depend on your age and the policy features you choose. The average period of disability is about three years.

INVESTING FOR RETIREMENT

Building Your Nest Egg

Your overall investment objective is to create wealth. You may want to save for a down payment on your first house, finance your kids' college educations, go on a luxury vacation, provide for a comfortable retirement, or achieve any number of other objectives. Each of your financial goals has a time frame that will influence your decision regarding the types of investments you choose. The shorter the time frame, the more conservative the investment should be. The longer the time frame, the more aggressive the investment can be.

Risk Tolerance and Asset Allocation

Before you can begin investing intelligently, you need to assess your risk tolerance. This is your ability to watch your investments decline in value in the short term because you believe they'll increase in the long term. The higher the risk, the greater the potential reward, and vice versa.

A Drawback of Low-Risk Investing

Low-risk investors face a significant potential downside: not having enough money for retirement. If you don't invest in stocks, you miss out on the most financially rewarding investment class. Historically, the stock market has always outperformed other investments (and the pace of inflation) over time, despite declines along the way.

If you can tolerate fluctuations in market value by focusing on the long term, consider investing in aggressive assets, such as stocks.

If you become nervous and uncomfortable when your investments suffer even a small decline in value, then conservative, low-risk choices are probably more your style.

High-risk investors are willing to take major risks in exchange for the possibility of substantial returns. They can still sleep at night even if they lose large amounts of money on paper (they don't actually lose any money until they sell off poorly performing investments). Moderate-risk investors are willing to take low to medium risks to increase their chances of investment growth. Conservative investors are uncomfortable at the thought of losing money in their investments and will give up the chance of high returns for the stability and safety of conservative investments with more predictable income. They are more concerned about losing money than they are about the potential for higher returns.

The highest-risk investments include:

- Futures
- Commodities
- Limited partnerships
- Collectibles
- Rental real estate
- Penny stocks (stocks that cost less than $5 per share)
- Speculative stocks (such as stock in new companies)
- Foreign stocks from volatile nations
- "Junk" (or high-yield corporate) bonds

Moderate-risk investments include:

- Growth stocks (companies that reinvest most of their profits to grow the business)
- Corporate bonds with lower (but still investment-grade) ratings
- Mutual funds or exchange-traded funds (ETFs)

- Real estate investment trusts (REITs)
- Blue chip stocks

  Limited-risk investments include:

- Top-rated investment-grade corporate and municipal bonds

  The lowest-risk investments include:

- Treasury bills and bonds
- FDIC-insured bank CDs (certificates of deposit)
- Money market funds

Practicing Wise Asset Allocation

Asset allocation means dividing up your portfolio among different types of assets to mitigate your overall investment risk. Wise allocation strategies help level out spikes and dips to keep your investments on a steadier path of growth and earnings. Different types of assets include stocks, bonds, cash equivalents (such as money market funds), and real estate. Aggressive asset allocation models hold substantially more stocks than other types of investments, focusing mainly on long-term growth opportunities. Conservative asset allocation involves a more balanced approach, where more stable holdings (such as bonds and cash equivalents) offset riskier stock investments.

Choosing what percentage to invest in each category depends on a number of factors, including your risk tolerance, your age, and how soon you expect to need the money. A popular rule of thumb used by some experts is to subtract your age from 110 or 120 to figure out how much of your investment portfolio should be invested in the stock market. For example, at age forty, you could invest 70 to 80 percent of your portfolio in stocks.

Diversify, Diversify, Diversify!

Diversification means not putting all your eggs in one basket. The more you spread out your investments among different kinds of securities and different sectors of the market (financial services, biomedical, technology), the lower the risk of substantial losses.

A well-diversified portfolio goes a step further than asset allocation. It refers to owning many different holdings within each asset type. For example, stock holdings would include small-cap, mid-cap, and large-cap stocks (more on this to follow), across many different industries, and possibly even international stocks. Usually when one sector or type of investment has low returns, another has high returns, so diversifying helps even out some of the ups and downs of the market.

When investing in cash equivalents, keep in mind that all cash equivalents are not the same. Even though there is a high expectation that cash equivalents are relatively risk-free, money market *funds* (as opposed to money market *accounts*) are not guaranteed by the government to retain their price. For example, in 2008, some of these funds, which were expected to hold steady at $1 per share, actually slipped to less than $1 per share (or "broke the buck") when investors withdrew their shares in droves in the wake of the financial crisis. The government did step in temporarily to guarantee these accounts but this guarantee no longer exists.

INVESTING IN STOCKS

Stocks are pieces of corporations; when you buy a stock, you are buying one share of a company. The value of your share rises and falls as the company's value changes.

Publicly owned companies sell shares of stock to raise money for operations or business expansion, invest in new technology or equipment, or meet other financial needs. Then, those shares get resold on the open market through the stock exchanges (such as the NYSE and the NASDAQ).

When stock prices go down, you don't actually lose any money unless you sell while the price is low. A loss that is only on paper can be recouped if the stock price rebounds, but selling locks in your loss and makes it final. It's important not to be scared into selling your stock holdings prematurely. You must understand what you are investing in so that you can determine whether a decrease in stock price represents an opportunity to buy more shares "on sale" or whether something has fundamentally changed within the company that may cause you to rethink your position.

When a stock price gets so high that investors are reluctant to buy, the company may declare a stock split. With a two-for-one split, you receive a free share of stock for every share you own, and the price per share is cut in half. The value of your total investment doesn't change, since there is twice the amount of shares in the company available for purchase, but the lower price may make it more attractive to investors and demand for the stock may actually increase the price as soon as the stock split is announced. Since you have more shares, your investment would be worth more once the price starts to increase than it would have been without the split.

Risk Level of Stocks

Stocks don't offer a guaranteed return, so don't ever invest in something you don't understand. Making an informed decision to assume risk creates an opportunity for a greater return on your investment. Jumping into investments you know nothing about, or that you hope will create a quick profit, puts your money at risk.

Stock Indexes

A stock index reports changes in prices for the market that it tracks. There are many US and international stock indexes, but the best known in the world is the Dow Jones Industrial Average (DJIA), which tracks thirty US blue chip stocks. Blue chips are the stocks of very large, well-established companies (in poker, the blue chips are the ones with the highest dollar value).

Other US indexes include the S&P 500, an index of the 500 largest companies in America; the Russell 2000, which measures the overall performance of small- to mid-cap companies; and the Wilshire 5000, which tracks the entire stock market. It's helpful to compare the performance of your stock, ETF, or mutual fund to the applicable index. If you have a small-cap mutual fund, for example, compare its performance to the Russell 2000. If the fund consistently underperforms the index, consider selling your shares and putting the money in a performance Russell 2000 index fund.

How to Buy Stocks

You can buy stocks through a full-service brokerage or a discount brokerage by calling a stockbroker and placing an order, or you can use a discount Internet broker such as Charles Schwab (www.schwab .com), TDAmeritrade (www.tdameritrade.com), or E*TRADE (www .etrade.com) to execute your own orders. Make sure you understand all of the terms on the online form before finalizing your purchase. You don't need a full-service broker unless you want advice regarding which stocks you should buy. Since brokers are paid on commission, they stand to gain financially from their recommendation; you should make up your own mind about what to buy or sell. Don't buy on a broker's recommendation alone.

Another way to buy stocks is through a direct stock purchase plan (DSPP), where you buy shares directly from the issuing company. There is little or no up-front cost and you will have the shares registered in your name. Some of the most well-known companies—such as Amazon.com ($250 minimum), Cisco Systems ($500 minimum, or $50 with recurring investment), Microsoft ($250 minimum, or $25 with recurring investment), Costco ($250 minimum, or $25 with recurring investment), and McDonalds ($500 minimum, or $50 with recurring investment)—can be bought this way.

Another option: Many companies offer dividend reinvestment plans (DRIPs). Corporations often pay out part of their earnings as dividends to shareholders, usually quarterly. The dividend can be paid in cash or stock. With a DRIP, you can reinvest the dividends in additional shares of stock, often without paying a commission. When the stock price goes up, so does the value of your reinvested shares. Be aware that the dividends are taxable no matter which form you receive; you will have to pay taxes on reinvested dividends.

When making investment choices, especially those involving individual stocks, heavily consider those companies that have a long history of paying dividends to their shareholders, and tend to increase those payouts every year. Dividends are discretionary distributions of a corporation's earnings made by its board of directors to its shareholders. A solid dividend-paying history lets you know that the corporation is both profitable and cash-rich, and a history of dividend growth instills confidence that it will stay that way.

Current income tax laws favor certain dividend income (known as qualified dividend income) received by shareholders, as it is subject to a lower tax rate than other forms of income (such as salaries, interest, or rents). Those qualified dividends get taxed at more favorable capital gains rates.

INVESTING IN BONDS

Bonds are known as fixed-income securities because their income is fixed at the time the issuer sells them. When you buy a bond, you're lending the bond issuer money in exchange for a fixed rate of return in the form of interest. The issuer usually pays the interest semiannually. With some types of bonds, though, the issuer pays all of the interest when the bond matures along with the principal it borrowed from you. Either way, you'll be taxed on the interest every year.

Bond Ratings

Bonds are rated for safety by bond-rating companies and given a grade between AAA (low risk) and C (high risk) to indicate the likelihood that the issuer will pay the interest and principal as promised. Each issuer has a slightly different grading system, so make sure you know which rating you are looking at. You can find bond ratings online at A.M. Best (www.ambest.com), Moody's (www.moodys.com), and Standard & Poor's (www.standardandpoors.com).

Corporations, states, cities, and governments all issue bonds for the same reason companies issue stock: to raise money for operations, expansion, or other financial needs.

Risk Level of Bonds

Bonds issued by the federal government are considered to be extremely safe, meaning there's virtually no risk that the bondholders won't receive their interest and principal payments. Some corporate bonds are safe, while others come with a higher risk. High-yield bonds pay a higher interest rate, but their nickname of "junk bonds" should give you fair warning of their risk; these bonds come with the very real risk that interest payments will not be made and the bonds will not be paid at maturity.

One of the risks associated with bonds—interest rate risk—considers relative interest rates (sometimes called coupon rates). If you lock in your money for a number of years at a fixed-interest rate, you may not be able to sell the bond for full price if other bonds are paying higher interest rates. Plus, with your money tied up in a lower-rate bond, you'd miss out on the opportunity to buy new bonds with higher interest rates.

Many bonds trade on the open market like stocks, though most transactions go through bond dealers. Generally, if market rates of interest go up, the value of bonds already issued will decline. Should market rates of interest go down, then the old bond with a higher interest rate will increase. These scenarios only matter when you're trading bonds, not if you're holding bonds until maturity.

Municipal bonds are issued by states and cities to fund projects such as road repairs, bridge building, park renovations, and any number of other projects requiring large amounts of money. You should exercise caution when considering this alternative, as most states are currently operating in a deficit position. The main attraction of state and local bonds is that their earnings are exempt from federal income tax, which makes them attractive to people in a high tax bracket. Likewise, US Treasury interest is exempt from state and local income taxation. Should you purchase a state or local bond from the state where you reside, you will find that the interest on the bond will be exempt from federal, state, and local income taxation. That is why they are often called "triple tax-free." Because of that tax benefit, it generally does not make sense to hold municipal bonds in tax-deferred retirement accounts.

How to Buy Bonds

You can buy individual federal government bonds, including US savings bonds, directly from the US Treasury, and both government and corporate bonds through a broker. Most bonds have $1,000 face values, meaning they originally sell for $1,000 (or close to that) each. That can make it tough for people to invest in individual bonds, especially if they want to diversify their holdings.

The easier option: Invest in a bond mutual fund or ETF, which invests in a large number of different bonds. You may incur fund expenses that will decrease your net return, but you can invest with much less money to start, and will have much more flexibility when it comes time to sell.

US Treasury Securities

US Treasury securities (bills, notes, and bonds) can be bought and sold in the securities market. They typically provide steady income and security. Treasury bills (or T-bills) mature four weeks to one year from their issue date. You buy them for less than their face value (called a discount to par), and you receive full face value when they mature. Treasury notes pay a fixed rate of interest every six months until maturity, which is from two to ten years. Treasury bonds also come with fixed biannual interest payments and mature in thirty years.

Treasury Inflation-Protected Securities (TIPS)

TIPS work like US Treasury bonds, except that the principal amount may be adjusted every six months by any subsequent increase in the Consumer Price Index (CPI), which is the US government's chief barometer of inflation. Any subsequent decrease may reduce the principal amount, but not below its original face value. Since the interest rate is determined as a percentage of the principal, any increase to the principal will bring about a corresponding increase in interest. The original interest rate on a TIPS may be somewhat lower than a US Treasury bond that has a fixed rate of interest throughout its term. TIPS are issued in terms of five, ten, and thirty years.

MUTUAL FUNDS

Mutual funds are a way for investors to pool their money so they can invest in many different stocks or bonds. Mutual funds are among the best alternatives for most people for several reasons:

- They automatically diversify your portfolio.
- They require only a small amount of money (compared to building a portfolio of individual stocks or bonds) to get started, possibly as little as $25 to $100.
- They're easy to track (easier than tracking dozens of individual holdings).

Like other types of investments, some mutual funds are riskier than others, so be sure to read the fund's objectives and know what it invests in. Will your money be buying stocks in blue chip companies or in the corporations of developing countries?

Although past performance is no guarantee of the future, look at how the fund has done over the last several years and compare it to an applicable index to see if it kept pace with its competitors. Also consider the expense ratio (the costs of owning the fund). Many mutual funds, especially managed funds, have relatively high expense ratios. Index funds typically offer the lowest fund expenses. The lower the expense ratio, the more of your earnings you get to pocket. You can find thorough mutual fund comparisons online at www.morningstar.com.

Risk Level of Mutual Funds

Mutual funds are less risky than individual stocks because their investment in any one stock is relatively small compared to their entire holdings. If one company takes a nosedive, the effect on the fund is usually minimal, or at least diluted. When entire sectors, such as technology stocks, head downhill, the impact can be great if the fund is heavily invested in technology stocks. The type of fund and its holdings determines the risk level.

Income versus Growth

Different funds have different investment objectives. Funds whose objective is current income invest heavily in bonds and dividend-paying stocks because of the steady income they generate. These funds appeal to retirees and those on a fixed income. Funds whose objective is long-term growth invest in stock, other stock mutual funds, and real estate because those investments usually increase in value over time. Growth and income funds are a hybrid of these two types and invest in both kinds of securities.

Load and No-Load Funds

Load is a sales fee or commission charged by some mutual funds, and is usually stated as a percentage of the amount purchased or sold. Front-end loads are fees charged up front when you buy the fund so that the full purchase price will not be invested. Back-end loads are fees you pay when you sell the fund. If the load is 6 percent and you invest $2,000, the load will be $120; that means if you invest $2,000, you'll only receive $1,880 worth of mutual fund shares. Funds that don't charge front-end or back-end loads are called no-load funds. When choosing a mutual fund, consider the load, if any, and the annual expense ratio. These will reduce your return. If you buy a fund with a 6 percent load and a 2 percent expense ratio, you have to earn an 8 percent return the first year to just break even. Many investment websites will provide a comparison of the average load and expense ratios of the mutual fund type you are interested in. Whenever possible, choose no-load fund options with low expense ratios to minimize costs and maximize earnings.

Various Indices

The best-known index is Standard & Poor's 500 (S&P 500), which invests in the top 500 US stocks. The largest and best-known index stock fund is Vanguard 500 from The Vanguard Group. Index funds usually charge no loads and have very low expense ratios since they are not actively managed.

Index Funds

An index fund's objective is to match the return of a specified index by buying shares in each stock in that index. Because index funds don't require specialized management, they're able to charge much lower expenses (sometimes as low as zero). Index funds offer both broad and segmented market exposure for strong diversification. In addition, they typically have very low turnover (the investments inside the fund aren't traded frequently), which also minimizes fund costs.

Market Capitalization

Mutual funds are often classified based on the market capitalization of the companies they invest in because "cap" is one of the criteria investors look at when choosing funds. A company's market cap is calculated by multiplying the current stock price times the number of outstanding shares of stock. The categories are:

- **Large-cap funds:** Companies with market capitalization over $10 billion.
- **Mid-cap stock funds:** Companies with market capitalization of $2 to $10 billion.
- **Small-cap funds:** Companies with market capitalization of $250 million to $2 billion.
- **Micro-cap funds:** Companies with market capitalization of less than $250 million.

Experts consider the large-cap funds, such as Vanguard's 500 Index, the least volatile, and the smaller company funds the most volatile.

How to Buy Mutual Funds

You can use full-service or discount brokers to buy mutual funds, or you can buy directly from a family of mutual funds, such as Vanguard (www.vanguard.com) or Fidelity (www.fidelity.com). It usually takes about 15 minutes to set up your account online and start investing.

Exchange-Traded Funds (ETFs)

An ETF is a security that tracks an index, a commodity, or a basket of assets like an index fund, but trades like a stock on an exchange. ETFs experience price changes throughout the day and are sold on the secondary market like individual stocks, so that the purchase price might be at, above, or below its NAV (Net Asset Value) depending on the number of buyers and sellers interested in the particular ETF. ETFs typically have lower fees, more transparency, and greater trading flexibility than index mutual funds. Most major brokerages offer a wide variety of low-fee and no-fee ETFs. You can learn more about ETFs at www.investopedia.com.

INDEX

ABOUT THE AUTHOR

Alfred Mill has a deep interest in personal finance and economics. He is the author of *Personal Finance 101*, *Economics 101*, and *Social Security 101*.

ABOUT THE TECHNICAL EDITOR

Michele Cagan is a CPA, author, and financial mentor. As the technical editor on this title, she brings more than twenty years of experience in personal financial planning. Michele has written numerous articles and books about personal finance, investing, and accounting, including *The Infographic Guide to Personal Finance*, *Investing 101*, *Budgeting 101*, *Real Estate Investing 101*, *Stock Market 101*, and *Financial Words You Should Know*. In addition to her financial know-how, Michele has a not-so-secret love of painting, Star Wars, and chocolate. She lives in Maryland with her son, dogs, cats, and koi. Get more financial guidance from Michele by visiting SingleMomCPA.com.

LEARN TO CREATE—
AND STICK TO—A BUDGET
WITH THIS COMPREHENSIVE,
EASY-TO-UNDERSTAND GUIDE!